SSAT & ISEE Vocabulary

(SSAT <u>Middle</u> Level & ISEE <u>Lower/Middle</u> Level)

By

J Stone

<u>Copyright Notice</u>

Contents

How NOT to memorize words

Vocabulary plays a big part in the SSAT & ISEE exams.

A good vocabulary is inextricably linked to a good memory. To have a deep and wide vocabulary, a student needs a good memory.

The commonly accepted idea that more memorizing makes memorizing easier is **false**, and there is little truth in the popular figure of speech that likens the vocabulary memory to a muscle that grows stronger with use.

However, practice may result in an unconscious improvement in the Winning methods of memorizing.

By practice, a student comes to unconsciously discover and employ new **associative methods** in recording of facts, making them easier to recall, but we can certainly add nothing to the actual scope and power of retention.

Yet many books on memory training seek to develop the general ability to remember by incessant practice in memorizing particular words, just as one would develop a muscle by exercise.

The real cause of a poor vocabulary memory is Not the loss of retentiveness, but the loss of an intensity of interest.

It is the failure to form sufficiently large groups and complexes of **related ideas**, emotions and muscular movements associated with the particular fact to be remembered.

Winning Strategy to build Vocabulary quickly

We recall things by their **associations**. When you set your mind to remember any particular fact, your conscious effort should not be to vaguely *will*, that it shall be impressed and retained, but analytically and deliberately connect it with other facts already in your mind.

The student who "crams" for an examination makes no permanent addition to his knowledge. There can be no recall without association, and "cramming" allows no time to form associations.

If you find it difficult to remember a word, do not waste your energies in "willing" it to return.

Try to recall some other fact associated with it.

To improve your memory you must increase the number and variety of your mental associations.

When you learn new words, make sure you learn them in a context. It is much easier to **picture a sentence** rather than picture a word in isolation.

Here is the step-by-step method that you can use to learn words quickly:

1. Link the word you are trying to learn, to another **rhyming** word or phrase.
2. Create a sentence **linking** the two words
3. Create a **mental image** for the sentence.

When you create the mental image make sure it meets **one or more of the following criteria** so that it 'sticks'.

Note: *Creating an image that is memorable and 'sticky' is the* <u>Key</u> *to learning words quickly and effectively.*

1. OUT OF PROPORTION - In all your images, try to distort size and shape. You can imagine things much larger than their normal size or conversely, microscopically small.

e.g. The word 'fertile' rhymes with 'mile'

Word to learn: fertile

Rhyme: mile

'' The soil was so <u>fertile</u> that plants grew over a <u>mile</u>.''

A plant that is a mile long is certainly out of proportion, and an image with a plant reaching the sky is likely to stick easily.

2. SUBSTITUTION - You could visualize footballers kicking a television around a football pitch instead of a football, or pens growing on a tree instead of leaves.

Substituting an out of place item in an image increases the probability of recall.

e.g. The word 'adopt' rhymes with 'a top'

Word to learn: adopt

Rhyme: a top

"The boy <u>adopted</u> <u>a top</u> that he found on the street."

3. EXAGGERATION - Try to picture a very large quantity in your images.

e.g. The word 'ample' rhymes with 'sample'

Word to learn: ample

Rhyme: sample

"The doctor needs an <u>ample</u> <u>sample</u> of blood."

Taking such a large sample of blood will surely scare any patient!

4. MOVEMENT - Any movement or action is always easy to remember.
e.g. The word 'abrupt' rhymes with 'erupt'

Word to learn: abrupt
Rhyme: erupt

"The <u>abrupt</u> <u>eruption</u> of the volcano caught everyone by surprise."

Imagining hot lava coming out and people running to save their lives will ensure that you do not easily forget the picture.

5. HUMOR - The funnier, more absurd and zany you can make your images, the more memorable they will be.

e.g. The word 'coincidence' rhymes with 'coin dance'

Word to learn: coincidence
Rhyme: coin dance

"What a coincidence!" the coin dancers said in unison, "Where did you get that hat?"

Applying **multiple combination** of these five principles when forming your images will help make your mental associations truly outstanding and memorable.

At first, you may find that you need to **consciously apply** one or more of the five principles in order to make your pictures sufficiently ludicrous.

After a little practice however, you should find that applying the principles becomes an **automatic** and natural process.

The following words are the most common words appearing in the SSAT/ISEE test and account for a majority of the difficult words that you are likely to encounter.

Each word below is illustrated with a picture using the Vocabulary building strategies listed above.

The pictures are provided as suggestions, and if based on your experiences/preferences, you find that you can come up with an alternative cartoon idea, please go ahead and use that.

Pronunciation Guide

The syllable breaks shown in this book reflect the pronunciation of a single word in normal speech. However, this book does not use the International Phonetic Alphabet (IPA) for pronunciation. The IPA is not very easy to understand, it is mostly for scholars and linguists. To make it easier for you to read the pronunciation, we have used the spelled pronunciation of the words.

\-\ Hyphens are used to separate syllables in pronunciation transcriptions. In actual speech, of course, there is no pause between the syllables of a word. The stress marks (bold type) indicate the stressed syllable of the word, as shown in the example below.

Interesting (**in**-tr*uh*-sting)

For one syllable words, the stress is always on the vowel and not on the consonant(s). One syllable words cannot have two stresses.

We can only stress vowels and not consonants. There are more complicated rules as to where to place the stress of a word.

For two syllable words (nouns, adjectives) the stress is placed on the first syllable. For verbs the stress is placed on the last syllable.

Example:

Nouns: **PRES**ent, **EX**port, **TA**ble

Adjectives: **PRES**ent, **CLE**ver, **HAP**py

Verbs: pre**SENT**, ex**PORT**, be**GIN**

There are many two syllable words whose meaning and class change with the change in stress. The word *'present'*, for example is a two-syllable word. If we stress the first syllable, it is a noun (gift) or an adjective (opposite of absent). But if we stress the second syllable, it becomes a verb (to offer).

Use the pronunciation guide to help you pronounce a word by placing the stress on its bold syllable.

Words with Cartoons

abrupt: (*uh*-**bruhpt**) adjective

sudden or unexpected; brief to the point of rudeness; curt

- The school bus came to an **abrupt** stop at the bus station.
- The Principal is always **abrupt** when speaking to the children.

Synonyms: sudden, quick, hasty, blunt, curt.

Antonyms: gradual, patient, courteous, nice, kind.

Rhyme: erupt

''The <u>abrupt</u> <u>eruption</u> of the volcano caught everyone by surprise.''

absurd: (ab-**surd**) adjective

something which is obviously or utterly senseless, illogical or untrue

- The platypus is an **absurd** creature, it looks like a duck and a beaver put together.
- "Your dog ate your homework? That is **absurd**!" said Jimmy's teacher.

Synonyms: irrational, silly, senseless, ridiculous, goofy.

Antonyms: logical, sensible, rational, practical, realistic.

Rhyme: a bird

"It is <u>absurd</u> to think that a tortoise can outpace <u>a bird</u>."

abundant: (*uh-**buhn**-duh nt*) adjective

present in great quantity; more than adequate; over-sufficient

- The river has an **abundant** supply of fish.
- Flowers are **abundant** in the western fields during summer.

Synonyms: ample, bountiful, copious, generous.

Antonyms: depleted, insufficient, lacking, scarce.

Rhyme: bun with a dent

''Tom picked up a <u>bun with a dent</u> from his <u>abundant</u> supply of buns.''

abyss: (uh-**bis**) noun

a large deep hole that appears to have no bottom

- It is believed that there are large sea creatures living deep in the **abyss**.
- Staring at his homework, Jimmy wanted to throw it into an **abyss**.

Synonyms: gorge, hole, pit, depth, void.

Antonyms: shallow, close, summit, altitude.

Rhyme: a bus

''The driver fell asleep and the <u>bus</u> fell straight into the <u>abyss</u>.''

accuse: (uh-**kyooz**) verb

to charge with fault or crime

- Jane **accused** Jimmy of stealing her chocolate bar.
- It took the detective some time to gather evidence, to successfully **accuse** Pat of theft.

Synonyms: blame, charge, complain, incriminate.

Antonyms: defend, approve, protect, pardon.

Rhyme: excuse

"She <u>accused</u> her son of cutting down the tree. The child could make no <u>excuse</u>."

accustomed: (*uh-**kuhs**-tuh md*) adjective

customary; usual; habitual

- Barry is **accustomed** to the mess in his room; he barely notices it.
- Aliens are not **accustomed** to the rules of Earth.

Synonyms: acclimatized, acquainted, seasoned, used to.

Antonyms: unusual, unaccustomed, unfamiliar.

Rhyme: a costume

"The little boy got so <u>accustomed</u> to wearing his Spiderman <u>costume</u> that he went to school in it."

acquire: (*uh-**kwahyuh r***) verb

to come into possession or ownership, to get as one's own

- Once you **acquire** the skills to play the drums you can join the band.
- She has **acquired** cooking skills from her father.

Synonyms: come by, get, obtain, procure.

Antonyms: lose, forfeit, surrender, fail.

Rhyme: a choir

''Bob finally <u>acquired</u> the role to lead <u>a choir</u>.''

adhere: (ad-**heer**) verb

follow; believe in; stick to

- As a student you must **adhere** to the rules of the school.
- Glue makes the wallpaper **adhere** to the wall.

Synonyms: stick, observe, join, comply.

Antonyms: disobey, abandon, ignore, separate.

Rhyme: a deer

''A deer did not adhere to the rules and got chased by the lion when he got too close.''

adopt: (*uh*-**dopt**) verb

to choose or take as one's own

- "Let's **adopt** this puppy!" cried Mandy.
- It took Charlie's parents a long time to think about **adopting** another pet.

Synonyms: take, accept, follow, pick.

Antonyms: reject, disapprove, disown, discard.

Rhyme: a top

"The boy <u>adopted</u> <u>a top</u> that he found on the street."

affluent: (*af-loo-uh nt*) adjective

having an abundance of wealth, property, or other material goods;
prosperous; rich

- I have an **affluent** uncle who lives in a castle.
- The Adams are the most **affluent** family in this city.

Synonyms: wealthy, prosperous, rich, well-to-do.

Antonyms: poor, destitute, needy, impoverished.

Rhyme: fluent

''Being <u>affluent</u> does not guarantee that you are <u>fluent</u> in a foreign
language.''

aftermath: (*ahf-ter-math*) noun

something that results or follows from an event, especially
one of a disastrous or unfortunate nature; consequence

- The **aftermath** of the war left the country in disarray.
- Susie slid down the slide and bumped her head, the **aftermath** left her in tears.

Synonyms: impact, outcome, issue, consequences.

Antonyms: cause, origin, source, start.

Rhyme: path

"In the <u>aftermath</u> of being in the <u>path</u> of a tornado, they were reduced to living in a tent."

allocate: (*al*-uh-keyt) verb

to set apart for a particular purpose; assign or allot

- The teacher **allocated** a color to each team.
- The librarian **allocates** books to their respective shelves.

Synonyms: allot, assign, arrange, divide.

Antonyms: keep together, cluster, bunch.

Rhyme: locate

"They <u>allocated</u> a place for each animal but they couldn't <u>locate</u> the alligator."

allure: (*uh-lew r*) noun/verb

the quality of being attractive or fascinating (n.)
to attract or charm; tempt (v.)

- The smell of freshly baked cookies **allured** the children to the kitchen. (v.)
- For some kids, sweets hold no **allure.** (n.)

Synonyms: charm, glamor, attraction, entice, tempt, appeal.

Antonyms: deter, repel, dissuade, discourage.

Rhyme: lure

''A rich man <u>allures</u> everyone but a poor man can <u>lure</u> no one.'' (v.)

ally: (*al-ahy*) noun/ verb

a person or organization that helps another (n.)

side with or support (v.)

- If Francis wasn't an **ally** during the competition we wouldn't have won. (n.)
- ''**Ally** with me and we can win the race together.'' claimed Rory. (v.)

Synonyms: join, unite, partner, comrade.

Antonyms: rival, foe, adversary, split.

Rhyme: a lie

''Are they <u>allies</u> or is it just <u>a lie</u>?'' (n.)

ambition: (*am-**bish**-uh n*) noun

an earnest desire for some type of achievement or distinction, as power, honor, fame or wealth, and the willingness to strive for its attainment

- Alison's **ambition** is to be a lawyer when she grows up.
- Brian has always said his **ambition** is to be a pilot.

Synonyms: goal, aim, aspiration, desire.

Antonyms: aversion, dislike, disinterest, idleness.

Rhyme: a mission

''His <u>ambition</u> is to finish the game's <u>missions</u>.''

ample: (*am-puh l*) adjective

fully sufficient or more than adequate for the purpose or needs; plentiful; enough

- There is **ample** time to study for the test next week.
- Susan has **ample** time to do her school project.

Synonyms: abundant, wide, plenty, spacious.

Antonyms: cramped, meagre, scarce, insufficient.

Rhyme: sample

''The doctor needs an <u>ample</u> <u>sample</u> of blood.''

appeal: (*uh-**peel***) noun/verb

a serious, urgent or heartfelt request (n.)

to make a heartfelt request; be attractive or interesting (v.)

- The little boy made countless **appeals** to stay up for Santa Claus. (n.)
- Police are **appealing** for information about the incident. (v.)

Synonyms: attractiveness, seek, persuade, request.

Antonyms: denial, refusal, ugliness, refusal.

Rhyme: a meal

''The <u>meal</u> doesn't look very <u>appealing</u>.'' (v.)

apprehensive: (*ap-ri-**hen**-siv*) adjective

uneasy or fearful about something that might happen

- Sharon was **apprehensive** about petting a snake.
- After being bitten by a dog, Theo was **apprehensive** about having one as a pet.

Synonyms: afraid, concerned, doubtful, uncertain.

Antonyms: calm, certain, clear, unfearful.

Rhyme: expensive

"When the bill came after the <u>expensive</u> dinner, I was <u>apprehensive</u>."

arouse: (*uh-rouz*) verb

to stir to action or strong response; excite; awaken from sleep

- The giant **aroused** from his sleep when he heard the singing harp.
- Seeing fireflies in the field **aroused** a magical feeling in Jane.

Synonyms: stir up, awaken, provoke, stimulate.

Antonyms: calm, lull, appease, bore.

Rhyme: a house

''The haunted <u>house</u> <u>aroused</u> fear in me.''

aspire: (*uh-spahyuh r*) verb

to long, aim, or seek ambitiously; be eagerly desirous, especially for something great or of high value

- Thomas has always **aspired** to be a pilot since he was a little boy.

- Janet **aspires** to be the class president.

Synonyms: dream, pursue, strive, aim.

Antonyms: dislike, despise, loll, accede.

Rhyme: empire

''The wicked king <u>aspired</u> to enlarge his <u>empire</u>.''

asunder: (*uh-**suhn**-der*) adverb

into separate parts; in or into pieces

- Sometimes it is easier to put together than to put **asunder.**

- Tommy kicked the ball so hard that it split the neighbor's door **asunder**.

Synonyms: apart, in pieces, split, separated.

Antonyms: together, close, combined, along.

Rhyme: thunder

''He split the vase <u>asunder </u>and blamed it on the <u>thunder</u>.''

atrocious: (*uh-**troh**-shuh s*) adjective

extremely or shockingly wicked, cruel, or brutal;
shockingly bad or tasteless; dreadful; abominable

- "The grouch stole the presents? What an **atrocious** man!" cried Jane.
- Bobby is a rude boy with **atrocious** manners.

Synonyms: awful, rotten, bad, wicked.

Antonyms: good, magnificent, wonderful, compassionate.

Rhyme: vicious

"The bully was <u>vicious</u>. His behavior was <u>atrocious</u>."

banish: (*ban-ish*) verb

to expel from or relegate to a country or place by authoritative decree; condemn to exile

- "Beware!" said the King, "Robbers and thieves will be **banished** from the kingdom."

- The great wizard **banished** all the trolls from the country.

Synonyms: dismiss, dispel, drive away, exile.

Antonyms: accept, admit, allow, include.

Rhyme: punish

"He was <u>punished</u> by being <u>banished</u> from his country."

barren: (*bar-uh n*) adjective

unproductive; unfruitful; bleak and lifeless

- The farmers could not reap harvest from their **barren** land.
- The pyramids stand tall in the **barren** desert.

Synonyms: arid, parched, depleted, unfruitful.

Antonyms: damp, productive, fertile, useful.

Rhyme: bear run

"The <u>bear run </u>was held in the <u>barren</u> desert."

belligerent: (*buh-**lij**-er-uh nt*) adjective

of warlike character; aggressively hostile; bellicose

- The **belligerent** children were scolded by their teacher.
- The headmaster made the **belligerent** student stand in a corner.

Synonyms: combative, quarrelsome, mean, hot-tempered.

Antonyms: agreeable, kind, friendly, co-operative.

Rhyme: belly of a giant

"The <u>belligerent</u> dwarf kicked the <u>belly of a giant</u>."

bemused: (*bih-myoozd*) adjective

bewildered or confused

- When reading the essays written by students, the teacher usually wore a **bemused** look on his face.

- Johnny was **bemused** by a maths question on the test.

Synonyms: distracted, baffled, lost, befuddled, engrossed.

Antonyms: alert, bright, disinterested, unoccupied.

Rhyme: bruise

''The shape of the <u>bruise</u> <u>bemused</u> him.''

besiege: (*bih-seej*) verb

to crowd around; encircle; surround and harass

- The emperor ran away when his city was **besieged**.
- The great warrior crossed the Rubicon River to **besiege** the city of gold.

Synonyms: blockade, attack, encircle, trap, overwhelm.

Antonyms: rescue, release, emancipate, liberate.

Rhyme: bees

"The soldier was <u>besieged</u> by the bees."

betray: (*bih-trey*) verb

to deliver or expose to an enemy by treachery or disloyalty

- Brian placed a trap for Seth, his best friend, to **betray** him.

- The knight **betrayed** the kingdom when he let the enemies through the gates.

Synonyms: abandon, deceive, forsake, mislead, cheat.

Antonyms: aid, assist, help, be loyal.

Rhyme: tea tray

''The King was <u>betrayed </u>by his ministers who put poison in his <u>tea tray</u>.''

bewildered: (*bih-**wil**-derd*) adjective

completely puzzled or confused; perplexed

- ''Where are we Toto?'' asked Dorothy, rather **bewildered**.

- Johnny was so **bewildered** that he could not answer the teacher's questions.

Synonyms: perplexed, puzzled, stumped, uncertain.

Antonyms: aware, clear, oriented, understanding.

Rhyme: wilderness

''He was <u>bewildered</u> by the utter <u>wilderness</u> and did not know which way to go.''

brood: (*brood*) noun/verb

a family of birds or young animals produced at one hatching or birth (n.)

to think for a long time about things that makes you sad or worried (v.)

- "Stop **brooding**, Charlie! It was a prank." said Mandy when she saw him frown. (v.)

- The bird flew under the bridge to feed its **brood**. (n.)

Synonyms: young, progeny, worry, be annoyed, mope.

Antonyms: be happy, strengthen, be elated, rise.

Rhyme: mood

"You cannot be in a bad <u>mood</u> and <u>brood</u> over bad news when you have a family to look after." (v.)

burden: (*bur-dn*) noun

that which is carried; load

- It was not a light load of books to carry; he had a **burden** to carry to school.

- ''I cannot fly with such a heavy **burden**!'' shouted the eagle while carrying the pig.

Synonyms: anxiety, concern, difficulty, hardship.

Antonyms: advantage, aid, ease, happiness.

Rhyme: bird on

''Holding a big <u>bird on</u> your head can be a <u>burden</u>.''

calamity: (*kuh-**lam**-i-tee*) noun

a great misfortune or disaster

- The village was saved from the **calamity** of another war.
- Charlie's volcano project exploded and turned into a **calamity**.

Synonyms: misfortune, trial, hardship, mishap.

Antonyms: advantage, miracle, fortune, success.

Rhyme: call mighty

''He called his <u>mighty</u> friend for help when a <u>calamity</u> hit him.''

candor: (*kan-der*) noun

the state or quality of being frank, open and sincere in speech or expression

- Darren's **candor** made him the best Presidential candidate.
- His **candor** and enthusiasm made Mr Roberts one of the most popular teachers in school.

Synonyms: directness, fairness, frankness, honesty.

Antonyms: deceit, dishonesty, inequity.

Rhyme: candy

''The boy nearly lost his <u>candy</u> because he spoke with <u>candor</u>.''

charred: (*chahr-d*) adjective

partially burnt with black surface; scorched

- The waiter served us **charred** greens and steak.
- Sandy forgot the cookies in the oven and they got **charred**.

Synonyms: burnt, parched, scorched, seared.

Antonyms: raw, underdone.

Rhyme: charged

''He <u>charged</u> at the <u>charred</u> gates which broke easily.''

coarse: (*kowrs*) adjective

lacking in fineness or delicacy of texture or structure

- The secret path in the park has **coarse** gravel.
- Mandy stuck a comb in her little brother's **coarse** hair.

Synonyms: gruff, crude, rough, tacky.

Antonyms: delicate, smooth, pleasant.

Rhyme: horse

"The <u>horse</u> hurt himself running on the <u>coarse</u> sand."

coax: (*kohks*) verb

to attempt to influence by gentle persuasion; flatter; cajole

- Timmy **coaxed** his little sister to go into the woods with him.
- The witch **coaxed** little children with sweets and delights.

Synonyms: cajole, tempt, lure, influence.

Antonyms: discourage, repulse, dissuade, disgust.

Rhyme: coke

''The father <u>coaxed</u> his boy to have juice instead of <u>coke</u>.''

coincidence: (*koh-**in**-si-duh ns*) noun

a striking occurrence of two or more events at one time apparently by mere chance

- Peter met Sandy at the cinema by **coincidence**.

- ''The twins are wearing the same dress, what a **coincidence**!'' said Mandy.

Synonyms: conformity, union, accompaniment, concurrence.

Antonyms: difference, disconnection, mismatch, deviation.

Rhyme: coin dance

''What a coincidence!'' the coin dancers said in unison, ''Where did you get that hat?''

companion: (*kuh m-**pan**-yuh n*) noun

a person who is frequently in the company of, associates with, or accompanies another

- Bobby is always playing with his dog Snowy, they are inseparable **companions**.

- ''My dog is my best friend and **companion**.'' said Tommy.

Synonyms: buddy, comrade, playmate, pal.

Antonyms: enemy, foe, opponent, stranger.

Rhyme: camping onion

''The onions went <u>camping</u> with their friends and <u>companions</u>.''

compel: (*kuh m-**pel***) verb

to force or drive, especially to a course of action

- Bobby and Sandy both **compelled** the new kid in school to have lunch with them.

- I will **compel** Charlie to go to the library with me.

Synonyms: urge, enforce, coerce, pressure.

Antonyms: dissuade, discourage, stop, deter.

Rhyme: come pal

''The shy boy felt <u>compelled</u> to join in the dancing when all of his friends said, "<u>Come pal</u>!''

comprise: (*kuh m-**prahyz***) verb

to include or contain

- The winning team **comprised** John, Timmy and Carl.

- Five-star hotels **comprise** a lounge, swimming pool and gaming rooms.

Synonyms: compose, include, contain, constitute.

Antonyms: exclude, lack, need, fail.

Rhyme: prize

''He won the <u>prize</u> for the triathlon competition, which <u>comprises</u> three different races.''

concealed: (*kuh n-seel d*) adjective

to hide; withdraw or remove from observation; cover or keep from sight

- The secret path to the cave is **concealed** behind the bushes.
- Timmy made sure he had his candy bar **concealed** under his coat.

Synonyms: bury, guard, cover, obscure.

Antonyms: disclose, expose, reveal, uncover.

Rhyme: sealed

''He <u>sealed</u> the ice cream cones and <u>concealed</u> them.''

conceited: (*kuh n-see-tid*) adjective

having an excessively favorable opinion of one's abilities or appearance

- The school's smartest student was **conceited** and refused to speak with other children.

- Mandy is unbearably **conceited**; she always talks about how beautiful she is.

Synonyms: arrogant, cocky, snotty, vain.

Antonyms: diffident, humble, meek, modest.

Rhyme: seated

"The Queen of Cones was <u>conceited</u> and refused to be <u>seated</u> with the peasants."

condemn: (*kuh n-dem*) verb

to express an unfavorable judgment on; indicate strong disapproval of; censure; punish

- The wicked Queen **condemned** the poor villagers to the dungeons.

- The judge **condemns** robbers and thieves to jail.

Synonyms: castigate, chide, criticize, decry.

Antonyms: approve, compliment, laud, praise.

Rhyme: conned them

''He is <u>condemned</u> because he <u>conned them</u>.''

confine: (*kon-fahyn*) verb

to enclose within bounds; limit or restrict

- The pirates found treasure **confined** in a chest.

- The animals in the zoo are **confined** in their cages.

Synonyms: cramp, imprison, detain, lock-up.

Antonyms: free, liberate, release, unlimited.

Rhyme: can't find

''Uncle Fred was <u>confined</u> at home when he <u>could not find</u> the keys.''

conspire: (*kuh n-spahyuh r*) verb

to agree together, especially secretly, to do something wrong, evil, or illegal

- The evil scientist **conspired** to take over the world.
- The bullies **conspired** together and set a trap for the other children.

Synonyms: collude, devise, connive, be in cahoots.

Antonyms: leave alone, neglect, disagree.

Rhyme: empire

''Enemies conspired to take over the empire.''

contemporary: (*kuh n-**tem**-puh-rer-ee*) adjective

existing, occurring, or living at the same time; belonging to the same time

- Michelangelo was a **contemporary** artist in his time.
- Robert's new book was not **contemporary**; it was a story about old times, of knights and princesses.

Synonyms: new, present-day, current, instant.

Antonyms: future, old, preceding, succeeding.

Rhyme: temporary

''The old bridge was <u>temporary</u> and would be replaced by something more <u>contemporary</u>.''

contempt: (*kuh n-**tempt***) noun

the feeling with which a person regards anything considered mean, vile, or worthless; disdain; scorn

- Her **contempt** for vegetables didn't stop her from eating pea soup.

- In his **contempt** for peasants, the king put all of them in prison.

Synonyms: antipathy, condescension, defiance, derision.

Antonyms: approval, esteem, flattery, honor.

Rhyme: tent

"The queen looked at the <u>tent</u> in <u>contempt</u> and refused to sleep in it."

conventional: (*kuh n-**ven**-shuh-nl*) adjective

conforming or adhering to accepted standards, as of conduct or taste

- Saving money in a piggy-bank is **conventional**.
- Writing letters is the **conventional** method for communicating.

Synonyms: current, ordinary, regular, traditional.

Antonyms: abnormal, different, extraordinary, irregular.

Rhyme: invention

''His <u>invention</u> broke <u>conventional</u> wisdom by enabling a dog to fly.''

convict: (*kon-vikt*) noun/verb

a person proved or declared guilty of an offense (n.)
to prove or declare guilty of an offense, especially after a legal trial (v.)

- **Convicts** in jail follow a strict timetable. (n.)

- To **convict** an innocent man to jail is unacceptable. (v.)

Synonyms: captive, felon, prisoner, culprit, jailbird.

Antonyms: victim, warden, release, acquit.

Rhyme: convince

''The judge <u>convinced</u> the <u>convict</u> to return the stolen goods.'' (n.)

correspond: (*kor-uh-spond*) verb

to be in agreement or conformity (often followed by with or to)

- Sally's dance movements **corresponded** to the beat of the music.

- Detective Watson was suspicious of Benny's story as it did not **correspond** with the report.

Synonyms: conform, compare, resemble, match.

Antonyms: mismatch, differ, clash, deviate.

Rhyme: pond

"Their stories of how the car got into the <u>pond</u> did not <u>correspond</u>."

covert: (*koh-vert*) adjective

concealed; secret; disguised

- Santa has only 24 hours to make **covert** trips to deliver all the presents.
- The boys are planning something **covert** for Halloween.

Synonyms: secret, hidden, disguised, incognito.

Antonyms: open, known, unconcealed, revealed.

Rhyme: convert

"The alien <u>converted</u> itself into a human to carry out <u>covert</u> actions."

covet: (*kuhv-it*) verb

to desire wrongfully, inordinately, or without due regard for the rights of others

- Imelda **covets** the crown on Aurora's head.

- One should not **covet** things that belong to others.

Synonyms: crave, envy, fancy, want.

Antonyms: dislike, hate, give.

Rhyme: comet

"Hailey <u>coveted</u> the discovery of his <u>comet</u>."

coy: (*koi*) adjective

artfully or affectedly shy or reserved; slyly hesitant; coquettish

- ''Oh, she's such a **coy** and reserved girl.'' said the teacher, ''She couldn't have shouted at her friends.''

- When asked about the secrets to the treasure, the pirate was **coy** about its whereabouts.

Synonyms: bashful, evasive, demure, prudish.

Antonyms: aggressive, immodest, forward, impudent.

Rhyme: toy

''The big boy is <u>coy</u> about his new <u>toy</u>.''

curb: (*kurb*) noun/verb

a check or restraint on something (n.)
to control; to restrain (v.)

- The government introduced tougher **curbs** on smoking. (n.)

- Tommy couldn't **curb** his excitement on Christmas morning. (v.)

Synonyms: restraint, limitation, barrier, restriction.

Antonyms: freedom, encourage, support, opening.

Rhyme: herb

''He used <u>herbs</u> to <u>curb</u> his appetite.'' (v.)

curt: (*kurt*) adjective

rudely brief in speech or abrupt in manner

- **Curt** replies are not the mark of a gracious person.
- ''Stop bothering me!'' said Mandy **curtly**.

Synonyms: offhand, blunt, terse, snippy.

Antonyms: tactful, civil, gracious, polite.

Rhyme: hurt

''I was <u>hurt</u> by her <u>curt</u> refusal to share her toys.''

curtail: (*ker-teyl*) verb

to reduce, limit, or stop something

- Due to heavy rains the farmers **curtailed** the time to harvest their lands.

- We **curtailed** our stay at the expensive hotel.

Synonyms: decrease, shorten, lessen, reduce.

Antonyms: lengthen, stretch, extend, prolong.

Rhyme: curved tails

''We were scared of the <u>curved tails</u> of the scorpions so we quickly <u>curtailed</u> our visit.''

debrief: (*dee-breef*) verb

to question someone in detail about work they have done for you

- Police Commissioner Jones **debriefed** Detective Hobbs on the new case.
- The enemy was caught and **debriefed** by soldiers.

Synonyms: interrogate, examine, grill, interview.

Antonyms: answer, reply, respond, feedback.

Rhyme: chief

''The chief debriefed the soldiers on the plan of attack.''

deceive: (dih-**seev**) verb

to make someone believe something that is not true

- The Princess was **deceived** by the witch's kindness.
- "Appearances can **deceive**", said the wise man.

Synonyms: cheat, defraud, trick, dupe.

Antonyms: guide, deliver, advise.

Rhyme: receive

''He <u>deceived</u> the teacher and <u>received</u> detention.''

defy: (*dih-fahy*) verb

to challenge the power of; resist boldly or openly

- "You dare **defy** me!" bellowed the King when the soldiers refused to march.

- The students **defied** the teacher's orders and ran around the classroom.

Synonyms: confront, disregard, elude, flout.

Antonyms: aid, assist, flatter, help.

Rhyme: deep fry

"The courageous young man <u>defied</u> the danger of death from the <u>deep fryer</u>."

demolished: (*dih-**mol**-ish d*) verb

to destroy or ruin (a building or other structure), especially on purpose; tear down; raze

- Most of the houses were **demolished** in the earthquake.

- The old school was **demolished** to make way for a library.

Synonyms: crush, ruin, wreck, break.

Antonyms: build, construct, raise, restore.

Rhyme: demon lashed

''The <u>demon lashed</u> the house and <u>demolished</u> it.''

depot: (*dep-oh*) noun

a place where trains, trucks or buses are kept or goods stored

- All the busses are parked at the **depot** at the end of the day.

- This town has no **depot** for trains.

Synonyms: garage, store, yard, terminal.

Antonyms: There are no antonyms for Depot.

Rhyme: pot

''The garden <u>depot</u> was overflowing with <u>pots</u>.''

derelict: (*der-uh-likt*) adjective/noun

in poor condition as a result of disuse and neglect (adj.)
person without a home, job or property (n.)

- The **derelict** man was taken to a shelter. (n.)

- There is a **derelict** house deep in the woods. (adj.)

Synonyms: delinquent, slack, irresponsible, lax.

Antonyms: careful, caring, improved, inhabited.

Rhyme: deer licked

''The <u>deer licked</u> the <u>derelict</u> man to try to awaken him.'' (n.)

despair: (*dih-spair*) noun/verb

complete loss of hope (n.)
to lose or be without hope (v.)

- The policeman told the woman not to **despair** when she lost her bag. (v.)

- Amy was in **despair** when she lost her teddy. (n.)

Synonyms: anguish, misery, sorrow, pain.

Antonyms: happiness, cheer, joy, pleasure.

Rhyme: disappear

"The boy was in <u>despair</u> when his kite <u>disappeared</u> in the sky." (n.)

despise: (*dih-spahyz*) verb

to regard with contempt, distaste, disgust, or disdain; scorn; loathe

- The villagers **despised** their king for his wickedness.
- ''I **despise** you, let me out!'' yelled the Princess when the evil witch locked her in the tower.

Synonyms: abhor, deride, detest, disdain.

Antonyms: accept, admire, adore, approve.

Rhyme: spice

''She despised the spicy food because it was too hot.''

devote: (*dih-**voht***) verb

to concentrate on a particular pursuit, occupation, purpose, cause

- Athletes **devote** all of their time to practice for the Olympics.

- Every day Thomas **devotes** an hour of his time to helping his sister learn how to ride a bicycle.

Synonyms: allot, dedicate, consign, give.

Antonyms: waste, accept, ignore.

Rhyme: goat

''The goat was devoted to being fit, and so ran every day.''

diminish: (*dih-**min**-ish*) verb

to become less, or to make something become less

- Not knowing answers will not **diminish** your intelligence.

- Even though she was hurt, it did not **diminish** her excitement about the race.

Synonyms: abate, curtail, decline, decrease.

Antonyms: develop, enlarge, expand, increase.

Rhyme: finish

''The crowds <u>diminished</u> as the concert <u>finished</u>.''

disarray: (*dis-uh-**rey***) noun/verb

a state of disorder or untidiness (n.)
throw into a state of disorder or untidiness (v.)

- The teacher told the children to tidy the **disarrayed** classroom. (v.)

- Tommy's room is always in such **disarray**. (n.)

Synonyms: shambles, clutter, jumble, untidiness.

Antonyms: tidiness, neatness, arrangement, order.

Rhyme: birthday

''After the birthday party the room was in disarray.'' (n.)

disheveled: (*dih-shev-uh ld*) adjective

untidy, disordered

- Jimmy looked **disheveled** coming out from the ditch that he had fallen into.
- The young man's hair was long and **disheveled.**

Synonyms: untidy, rumpled, unkempt, messy.

Antonyms: tidy, neat, groomed, pristine.

Rhyme: the devil

''The devil looked disheveled.''

dismay: (*dis-mey*) noun/verb

to break down the courage of completely, as by sudden danger or trouble; dishearten thoroughly; daunt (v.)
sudden or complete loss of courage; utter disheartenment (n.)

- My mother was **dismayed** to learn that my brother and I had lied. (v.)

- To his **dismay**, he missed the last train. (n.)

Synonyms: anxiety, apprehension, dread, upset.

Antonyms: assurance, calm, composure, delight.

Rhyme: This may

"<u>This may</u> mean we have lost the race." she said with <u>dismay</u>." (n.)

disperse: (*dih-spurs*) verb

to separate and move apart in different directions without order or regularity; become scattered

- Jane pinched her nose and waved her hand to **disperse** the foul smell.

- The city police told the crowd to **disperse**.

Synonyms: dispel, disband, scramble, dismiss.

Antonyms: accumulate, gather, assemble, unite.

Rhyme: purse

''Swinging her <u>purse</u> she made the gang <u>disperse</u>.''

dispute: (*dih-**spyoot***) noun/verb

a disagreement or argument (n.)
to argue or quarrel about something (v.)

- The pigeons at the square **disputed** over crumbs of bread. (v.)
- Tom and Jane are always having a **dispute** as to who should clean up after dinner. (n.)

Synonyms: bickering, brawl, debate, quarrel.

Antonyms: calm, agreement, peace, quiet.

Rhyme: flute

''There's a dispute over the flute.'' (n.)

distinct: (*dih-stingkt*) adjective

distinguished as not being the same; not identical; separate
(sometimes followed by *from*)

- Coal is **distinct** from diamonds even though they are the same.

- Mandy and Sally both heard the **distinct** sound of a growl from inside their tent.

Synonyms: definite, clear, noticeable, specific.

Antonyms: indefinite, obscure, uncertain, vague.

Rhyme: link

"The <u>distinct</u> islands were <u>linked</u> by bridges."

distress: (*dih-**stres***) noun/verb

great pain, anxiety or sorrow (n.)
cause someone pain, anxiety or sorrow (v.)

- Timmy is waiting in **distress** at the dentist's office. (n.)

- Johnny was **distressed** after seeing his test results. (v.)

Synonyms: anguish, worry, anxiety, sorrow.

Antonyms: delight, happiness, pleasure, cheer.

Rhyme: press

"In her <u>distress</u>, she kept <u>pressing</u> the wrong button and could not get help." (n.)

docile: (*doh-sahyl*) adjective

easily managed or handled; tractable

- Charlie's little sister is a sweet and **docile** girl.

- Timmy took home a **docile** puppy from the street.

Synonyms: easy-going, gentle, well-behaved, humble.

Antonyms: determined, stubborn, headstrong, obstinate.

Rhyme: dose I'll

"The <u>dose I'll</u> give him will make him more <u>docile</u>."

dormant: (*dawr-muh nt*) adjective

in a state of rest or inactivity; inoperative; in abeyance

- After being **dormant** for many years, the volcano started to rumble.

- During winter many insects lie **dormant**.

Synonyms: asleep, inert, comatose, lethargic.

Antonyms: active, alert, awake, conscious.

Rhyme: roar meant

''The lion's <u>roar meant</u> the sleeping bear could not afford to remain <u>dormant</u>.''

dose: (*dohs*) noun

an amount of something, often something unpleasant

- Mary came into the office with a **dose** of bad news for her boss.

- The new story had a good **dose** of mystery in its plot.

Synonyms: measure, shot, portion, quantity.

Antonyms: estimate, approximate.

Rhyme: gross

''The <u>dose</u> of medicine tasted <u>gross</u>.''

drought: (*drout*) noun

a period of dry weather, especially a long one that is injurious to crops

- The nearby river dried up and brought **drought** to the land.
- The animals were all thirsty during the **drought**.

Synonyms: dry spell, dehydration, parchedness, dearth.

Antonyms: excess, monsoon, wetness, plenty.

Rhyme: sprout

"The sprout did not survive the drought."

dwelling: (*dwel-ing*) noun

a building or place of shelter to live in; place of residence; abode; home

- The lion's **dwelling** is its den.
- Billy the goat went to the trolls' **dwelling** under the bridge.

Synonyms: habitat, residence, house, quarters.

Antonyms: homeless.

Rhyme: selling

''The family is <u>selling</u> their <u>dwelling</u>.''

economize: (*ih-**kon**-uh-mahyz*) verb

spend less; avoid waste or extravagance

- We should always **economize** so that we can save for a rainy day.

- Sandy **economized** and now she has bought herself a bicycle.

Synonyms: conserve, cut down, save, scrimp.

Antonyms: spend, squander, throw away, waste.

Rhyme: hypnotize

''The only way he could think of, to make her <u>economize</u>, was to <u>hypnotize</u> her.''

elude: (*ih-lood*) verb

to avoid or escape by speed, cleverness or trickery; evade

- Billy took a shortcut to **elude** the bully.

- David **eluded** the giant and hit him with a stone.

Synonyms: evade, flee, outrun, eschew.

Antonyms: confront, meet, face, encounter.

Rhyme: dude

''The masked <u>dude</u> <u>eluded</u> the police.''

employ: (*em-ploi*) verb

to hire or engage the services of (a person or persons); provide employment for; have or keep in one's service

- James wants to be **employed** by a secret service agency.

- Sandy needs to **employ** someone to help her in the bakery.

Synonyms: hire, engage, recruit, appoint, enlist.

Antonyms: dismiss, unemployed.

Rhyme: cowboy

''The movie director wants to <u>employ</u> a <u>cowboy</u>.''

endeavor: (*en-**dev**-er*) noun/verb

an attempt to achieve a goal (n.)
try hard to do or achieve something (v.)

- Neil the scientist, **endeavored** to fly to the moon. (v.)

- Charlie's teachers wished him the best for his future **endeavors**. (n.)

Synonyms: venture, enterprise, undertaking, work.

Antonyms: inactivity, pastime, laziness, idleness.

Rhyme: would never

"His <u>endeavor</u> to fly <u>would never</u> be successful." (n.)

endure: (*en -dyoo r*) verb

to hold out against; sustain without impairment or yielding; undergo

- Janet had to **endure** the pain in her legs while she climbed up the mountain.

- Lost in the woods, the children had to **endure** hunger.

Synonyms: brave, encounter, experience, go through.

Antonyms: disallow, halt, hide, refuse.

Rhyme: injure

''He had to <u>endure</u> the pain when he was <u>injured</u>.''

enterprise: (*en-ter-prahyz*) noun

a company or business; a project or undertaking (especially a bold or complex one)

- The carpenter lost his woodwork **enterprise** to termites.

- Amy is rich because of her cupcake **enterprise**.

Synonyms: project, business, trade, establishment.

Antonyms: unemployment, idleness, inaction.

Rhyme: French fries

''He started the <u>enterprise</u> by selling <u>French fries</u>. ''

entice: (*en-tahys*) verb

to lead on by exciting hope or desire; allure

- The knight was **enticed** by the prize in the tournament.

- Billy tried to **entice** the troll under the bridge with a cookie.

Synonyms: coax, attract, tempt, lure.

Antonyms: repel, repulse, disenchant, dissuade.

Rhyme: dice

''The clatter of the rolling <u>dice</u> <u>enticed</u> him back to the table.''

erect: (*ih-rekt*) adjective/verb

upright in position or posture (adj.)
put together and set upright (verb)

- People still wonder how the ancient Egyptians **erected** the pyramids. (v.)

- We stood very **erect** and still, as the big dog approached. (adj.)

Synonyms: elevated, firm, raised, standing.

Antonyms: lowered, prone, prostrate, level.

Rhyme: wrecked

''The storm <u>wrecked</u> the tents but the campers quickly <u>erected</u> them again.''

evoke: (*ih-**vohk***) verb

to call up or produce (memories, feelings)

- The evil witch **evoked** a spell and put Princess Pea into a deep slumber.
- The dragon in the mountain **evoked** a sense of fear in the hearts of the villagers.

Synonyms: arouse, conjure, elicit, awaken.

Antonyms: calm, repress, stifle, suppress.

Rhyme: awoke

''The nightmare <u>evoked</u> a sense of fear and he <u>awoke</u> frightened.''

excerpt: (*ek-surpt*) noun

a passage or quotation taken or selected from a book, document, film, or the like; extract

- After reading an **excerpt** of the new book, Amy decided not to buy it.

- The famous author read an **excerpt** from her new book.

Synonyms: extract, fragment, piece, portion.

Antonyms: all, entirety, whole, totality.

Rhyme: expert

''The film <u>expert</u> could recognize a film even from a very short <u>excerpt</u>.''

excess: (*ek-ses*) adjective/noun

more than what is necessary, usual, or specified (adj.)
an amount that is more than enough; overconsumption (n.)

- The airline charged us extra for **excess** baggage. (adj.)

- The rich man lived a life of **excess**. (n.)

Synonyms: fat, overload, plenty, surplus.

Antonyms: lack, scarcity, few, little.

Rhyme: success

''He was <u>successful</u> in losing his <u>excess</u> weight after he started running regularly.'' (adj.)

exclaim: (*ik-skleym*) verb

to cry out or speak suddenly and vehemently, as in surprise,
strong emotion, or protest

- ''He hit me first!'' **exclaimed** my sister as I broke up the fight
  between her and my brother.

- He **exclaimed** with glee when Superman turned up at his
  birthday party.

Synonyms: blurt, proclaim, call out, shout.

Antonyms: conceal, hide, refrain, be quiet.

Rhyme: blame

''He is to be <u>blamed</u> for the accident!'' the woman <u>exclaimed</u>.

exhilarating: (*ig-**zil**-uh-reyt ing*) adjective

making one feel happy, animated or elated; thrilling

- ''I will never ride a roller-coaster again but I must admit, it was **exhilarating**.'' said my sister.

- ''I am an adventurer and jumping out of planes is **exhilarating**.'' said Anna.

Synonyms: breath-taking, exciting, inspiring, intoxicating.

Antonyms: boring, depressing, unstimulating, discouraging.

Rhyme: accelerating

''There was nothing more <u>exhilarating</u> than <u>accelerating</u> her new sports car.''

extract: (*ek-strakt*) noun/verb

to get, pull, or draw out, usually with special effort, skill, or force (v.)

a solution or preparation containing the active principles of a drug, plant juice, or the like; concentrated solution (n.)

- I went to the dentist to get my tooth **extracted**. (v.)

- We brought back Vanilla **extract** from our holiday in Madagascar. (n.)

Synonyms: cull, derive, distil, elicit.

Antonyms: give, disperse, divide, fail.

Rhyme: cracked

"The careless nurse <u>cracked</u> the needle while <u>extracting</u> blood." (v.)

famine: (*fam-in*) noun

extreme and general scarcity of food, as in a country or a large geographical area.

- During the **famine** the good king gave his people food from the granary.

- All the animals were hungry during the **famine**.

Synonyms: drought, poverty, scarcity, dearth.

Antonyms: abundance, plenty, feast, supply.

Rhyme: farming

"The farmers couldn't keep <u>farming</u> during the <u>famine</u>."

fatal: (*feyt-l*) adjective

causing or capable of causing death; deadly

- The escaped zebra from the zoo caused a **fatal** accident on the highway.

- We must choose wild mushrooms carefully, some of them can prove to be **fatal**.

Synonyms: deathly, poisonous, fateful, destructive.

Antonyms: blessed, fortunate, harmless.

Rhyme: fat elf

''The <u>fat elf</u> jumped on the dragon, wounding it <u>fatally</u>.''

fatigue: (*fuh-teeg*) noun/verb

extreme tiredness from bodily or mental exertion (n.)
cause someone to feel exhausted (v.)

- **Fatigue** kept Bobby from concentrating in class. (n.)

- Sandy was **fatigued** by her long journey. (v.)

Synonyms: lethargy, weariness, exhaustion, tired.

Antonyms: energy, strength, freshness, alacrity.

Rhyme: football league

''The players were <u>fatigued</u> after winning the finals of the <u>football league</u>.'' (v.)

feeble: (*fee-buh l*) adjective

physically weak, as from age or sickness; frail

- The dragon on the mountain-top is old and **feeble** now.
- Billy helped the **feeble** old lady to cross the street.

Synonyms: ailing, frail, weak, helpless.

Antonyms: able, capable, healthy, strong.

Rhyme: eagle

''An <u>eagle</u> is not a <u>feeble</u> creature.''

feign: (*feyn*) verb

to represent fictitiously; put on an appearance of

- ''Stop **feigning** innocence!'', my brother yelled at me ''I knew you took my toy.''

- Cathy knew about the birthday party and **feigned** surprise when everyone shouted, ''Surprise!''

Synonyms: act, affect, assume, bluff.

Antonyms: be honest, be true, real, actual.

Homonyms: fain

Rhyme: pain

''The footballer <u>feigned</u> the <u>pain</u>.''

feint: (*feynt*) noun/verb

a deceptive or pretended blow, thrust or other movement, especially in boxing or fencing (n.)
make a deceptive or distracting movement, especially during a fight (v.)

- The retreat by the enemy was but a **feint** to get the Kingdom to open its doors. (n.)

- ''Did you **feint** a stomach ache to get out of doing P.E?'' asked my brother. (v.)

Synonyms: ruse, artifice, bait, bluff, cheat.

Antonyms: frankness, honesty, openness, truth.

Homonyms: faint

Rhyme: faint

''He <u>fainted</u> after he missed his opponent's <u>feint</u>.'' (n.)

fertile: (*fur*-tahyl) adjective

bearing, producing, or capable of producing vegetation, crops, abundantly; prolific

- Jack threw the beans out the window onto the **fertile** land below.

- We need **fertile** soil to grow more vegetables.

Synonyms: productive, arable, lush, bountiful, high-yielding.

Antonyms: barren, sparse, infertile, useless.

Rhyme: mile

''The soil was so <u>fertile</u> that plants grew over a <u>mile</u>.''

fleet: (*fleet*) adjective/noun

fast and nimble in movement (adj.)
group of ships or vehicles; a country's navy (n.)

- He owns a **fleet** of taxicabs. (n.)

- "Get me a **fleet** horse!" bellowed the king. (adj.)

Synonyms: speedy, brisk, fast, swift.

Antonyms: slow, sluggish, clumsy, tardy.

Rhyme: athlete

"The most <u>fleet</u> <u>athlete</u> won the race." (adj.)

flora: (*flohr-uh*) noun

the plants of a particular region or period, listed by species and considered as a whole

- The **flora** of the country changes throughout the seasons, it is most beautiful in spring.

- Island **flora** is exotic and very different from country **flora**.

Synonyms: vegetation, plant, botany, verdure.

Antonyms: fauna, organism, animal.

Rhyme: poorer

''The <u>flora</u> in the <u>poorer</u> soil doesn't grow well.''

flourish: (*fluhr-ish*) verb

to grow luxuriantly, or thrive in growth; wave something to attract attention

- My mother's rose garden **flourishes** under the sun.

- Watering your plants will make them **flourish**.

Synonyms: thrive, prosper, grow, bloom, brandish, wave.

Antonyms: shrink, shrivel, struggle, decline.

Rhyme: fish

''Keep the <u>fish</u> in the water, not on the floor, and they will <u>flourish</u>.''

foe: (*foh*) noun

a person who feels enmity, hatred or malice toward another; enemy

- Friend or **foe** I will help if help is needed.
- The **foe** of my foe is my ally.

Synonyms: enemy, opponent, adversary, rival.

Antonyms: friend, ally, accomplice, partner.

Rhyme: blow

''He felled his <u>foe</u> with a single <u>blow</u>.''

forbid: (*fawr-bid*) verb

to command (a person) not to do something, have something, or not to enter some place

- The principal **forbids** children from running in the school.
- My mother **forbade** me from eating chocolate before dinner.

Synonyms: ban, block, disallow, deny.

Antonyms: allow, admit, approve, encourage.

Rhyme: orbit

"We can't <u>forbid</u> the moon from <u>orbiting</u> the earth."

fragment: (*frag-muh nt*) noun/verb

a part broken off or detached (n.)
to break (something) into pieces or fragments; cause to disintegrate (v.)

- My mother swept up the **fragments** of the vase which I broke. (n.)

- The garden chair, already broken, **fragmented** under my aunt's weight as she sat down. (v.)

Synonyms: bit, chunk, lump, piece.

Antonyms: lot, whole, entirety, total.

Rhyme: frog

''There is not a <u>fragment</u> of truth in the <u>frog's</u> story!'' thought the princess. (n.)

fraught: (*frawt*) adjective

filled with (something undesirable)

- The forest by the lake is **fraught** with danger.

- Boxing is a sport that is **fraught** with bruises and injuries.

Synonyms: laden, filled, replete, loaded.

Antonyms: empty, barren, devoid, deficient.

Rhyme: fought

''The river was <u>fraught</u> with crocodiles, and although the explorer <u>fought</u> hard, he had to turn back.''

gene: (*jeen*) noun

a part of a cell that controls or influences the appearance, growth, of a living thing

- Scientists look at animal **genes** to help understand more about them.

- You can get a lot of information from the **genes** of an animal.

Synonyms: chromosome, heredity, genetic code, nucleic acid.

Antonyms: There are no antonyms for Gene.

Homonyms: jean

Rhyme: lean

''He seems to have got his <u>'lean'</u> <u>gene</u> from his father rather than from his mother.''

gnarled: (*nahrld*) adjective

bent or twisted, especially with age

- The wizard conjured a spell and raised his **gnarled** staff to the sky.

- My foot caught the **gnarled** root of the sycamore tree and I fell to the ground with a loud thud.

Synonyms: contorted, crooked, deformed, twisted.

Antonyms: straight, unbent, uncurled, untwisted.

Rhyme: walled

''The thousand year old <u>gnarled</u> tree was <u>walled</u> to protect it from wood cutters.''

grate: (*greyt*) verb

to reduce to small particles by rubbing against a rough surface or a surface with many sharp-edged openings; make an unpleasant sound

- ''Do we **grate** lemons for lemonade?'' asked Charlie's little sister.

- You need **grated** carrots to make carrot cake.

Synonyms: scrape, rasp, grind, chafe.

Antonyms: pacify, appease, gladden, placate.

Rhyme: grape

''You can't <u>grate</u> <u>grapes</u>.''

gratitude: (*grat-i-tyood*) noun

the quality or feeling of being grateful or thankful

- I helped my brother with his homework; in return he showed **gratitude** by letting me play with his toys.

- The students expressed their deep **gratitude** for the teachers' support.

Synonyms: appreciation, thankfulness, gratefulness, grace.

Antonyms: censure, ingratitude, condemnation, thanklessness.

Rhyme: great attitude

"Someone with <u>great attitude</u> shows <u>gratitude</u>."

grotesque: (*groh-**tesk***) adjective

odd or unnatural in shape, appearance, or character; very ugly or
absurd; bizarre

- After his life in the city, Nate finds old castles both **grotesque**
  and amazing.

- The **grotesque** ogres stole the farmer's sheep.

Synonyms: bizarre, weird, freakish, eerie.

Antonyms: beautiful, nice, pretty, regular.

Rhyme: grow tusks

''The thought of <u>growing tusks</u> is <u>grotesque</u>.''

hoax: (*hohks*) noun/verb

something intended to deceive or defraud (n.)
to deceive by a hoax; hoodwink (v.)

- The villagers soon found out that the stories about wolves were a **hoax**. (n.)

- Jeannie **hoaxed** her friends and played a prank on them. (v.)

Synonyms: bamboozle, bluff, deceive, con.

Antonyms: honest, good, real, sincere.

Rhyme: smoke

''The <u>smoke</u> was a <u>hoax</u>.'' (n.)

ignite: (*ig-nahyt*) verb

to set on fire; kindle

- Johnny's father **ignited** a match to get a fire going for the fireplace.
- As the lightening hit the tree, it **ignited** into flames

Synonyms: burn, flare up, inflame, fire.

Antonyms: cool, extinguish, put out, dull.

Rhyme: bright

''The <u>bright</u> sun helped us ignite the <u>fire</u>.''

ignorant: (*ig-ner-uh nt*) adjective

lacking knowledge or information as to a particular subject or fact

- Tom, a country boy, is **ignorant** of city life.

- **Ignorant** of the danger ahead the curious children went into the woods.

Synonyms: unknowing, untaught, uninformed, unaware.

Antonyms: aware, knowledgeable, cognizant, informed.

Rhyme: ignore ant

''They were <u>ignorant</u> of its presence and <u>ignored the ant</u>.''

immense: (*ih-mens*) adjective

immeasurable; boundless

- A super-hero has **immense** power to stop a super-villain.

- The Eiffel tower ought to be **immensely** heavy.

Synonyms: enormous, huge, gigantic, large.

Antonyms: miniature, little, small, tiny.

Rhyme: sense

''His wrestling opponent was so <u>immense</u> that it made no <u>sense</u> to fight him.''

impede: (*im-**peed***) verb

to retard in movement or progress by means of obstacles or hindrances; obstruct; hinder

- Any plan can be **impeded** in any way, at any time.

- The wise king **impeded** the enemy's attack on the city.

Synonyms: hinder, obstruct, block, thwart.

Antonyms: assist, support, facilitate, help.

Rhyme: centipede

''Their progress was <u>impeded</u> by the many <u>centipedes</u> in the swamp.''

impudent: (*im-pyuh-duh nt*) adjective

not showing due respect

- The signboard read: **Impudence** will not be tolerated in this school.

- I was sent to the principal's for **impudent** behavior.

Synonyms: brazen, cheeky, insolent, impertinent, audacious.

Antonyms: humble, modest, polite, retiring.

Rhyme: student

''The impudent student, always argued with the teacher.''

inaudible: (*in-**aw**-duh-buh l*) adjective

 unable to be heard

- The slow rumble of thunder was almost **inaudible**.

- A new-born puppy's cries are practically **inaudible**.

Synonyms: quiet, unhearable, imperceptible.

Antonyms: audible, hearable, loud, perceptible.

Rhyme: in a bell

''When you are <u>in a bell</u> everything else is <u>inaudible</u>.''

incision: (*in-sizh-uh n*) noun

a cut, gash or notch

- The doctor told me he would have to make an **incision** on my arm.
- While climbing a rock wall, the sharp edges made several **incisions** on my knees.

Synonyms: laceration, dissection, opening, gash.

Antonyms: closing, closure, solid, fill.

Rhyme: decision

''The doctor can't make a <u>decision</u> about where to make the <u>incision</u>.''

incite: (*in-sahyt*) verb

to stir, encourage, or urge on; stimulate or prompt to action

- The bully **incites** everyone to pick on someone smaller than them.

- The fire alarm **incited** panic and everyone was running around.

Synonyms: induce, agitate, trigger, encourage.

Antonyms: block, calm, dampen, depress.

Homonyms: insight

Rhyme: in sight

''The sleeping cat was <u>incited</u> to run as soon as the big dog came <u>in sight</u>.''

inconspicuous: (*in-kuh n-**spik**-yoo-uh s*) adjective

not clearly visible, not noticeable

- **Inconspicuous** to the eye, the eagle builds its nest high up on tree-tops.

- The robber was standing **inconspicuously** in a dark corner.

Synonyms: obscure, unobtrusive, invisible, unnoticed.

Antonyms: clear, conspicuous, noticeable, prominent.

Rhyme: spick and span

''I want it <u>spick and span</u>! You must clean off all the marks even the <u>inconspicuous </u>ones.'' said the manager to the cleaner.''

indulge: (*in-**duhlj***) verb

to yield to an inclination or desire; allow oneself to follow one's will (often followed by *in*)

- Tommy **indulged** in his favorite dessert.
- My sisters love to **indulge** in shopping sprees.

Synonyms: gratify, nourish, pamper, satiate.

Antonyms: deprive, dissatisfy, ignore, neglect

Rhyme: bulge

''Indulging in too many sweets can give you a bulge.''

inedible: (*in-ed-uh-buh l*) adjective

unfit to be eaten

- The burnt cookies were **inedible**.

- Not all berries are edible, some are poisonous therefore **inedible**.

Synonyms: uneatable, bad, bitter, rotten.

Antonyms: appetizing, delicious, edible.

Rhyme: incredible

''He ate the <u>inedible</u> dish <u>incredibly</u> fast because he was very hungry.''

inhabit: (*in-**hab**-it*) verb

to live or dwell in (a place), as people or animals

- Alligators **inhabit** river-bottoms and swampy areas.
- More than a billion people **inhabit** the country of China.

Synonyms: reside, occupy, dwell, live.

Antonyms: vacate, depart, leave, desert.

Rhyme: rabbit

''A <u>rabbit</u> doesn't usually <u>inhabit</u> a house.''

inspire: (in-**spahy***uh* r) verb

to fill with a creative influence or create a positive feeling; to inhale

- **Inspired** by the hero's bravery, the townspeople fought the enemies with him.

- What could have **inspired** the artist to paint such beautiful art in the 16th century?

Synonyms: stimulate, cause, influence, motivate.

Antonyms: bore, calm, dissuade, enervate

Rhyme: admire

''He <u>admired</u> the famous scientist so much that he was <u>inspired</u> to become one himself.''

interpret: (*in-**tur**-prit*) verb

to give or provide the meaning of; explain; explicate; elucidate

- Ella speaks many languages, she **interprets** English for tourists.
- Elton doesn't speak Turkish; he could not **interpret** when the tourist asked for directions.

Synonyms: clarify, construe, decipher, translate.

Antonyms: confuse, misunderstand, misinterpret, disbelieve.

Rhyme: interrupt

"The detective asked not to be <u>interrupted</u> when he was trying to <u>interpret</u> the code."

isolation: (*ahy-suh-ley-shuh n*) noun

the fact that something is separate and not connected to other things

- When no one is around I feel like I'm in **isolation**.

- A hermit lives away from society, in **isolation**.

Synonyms: seclusion, solitude, loneliness, detachment.

Antonyms: society, community, inclusion, company.

Rhyme: station

''I was scared to go to the railway <u>station</u> because it was very <u>isolated</u>.''

justify: (*juhs-ti-fahy*) verb

to defend or uphold as warranted or well-grounded

- Benny tried to **justify** the reason for fighting with the bully.

- The lawyer tried to **justify** his client's actions in court.

Synonyms: condone, defend, explain, advocate.

Antonyms: attack, condemn, contradict, deny

Rhyme: just a fly

Monk: "You cannot <u>justify</u> murder."

Man: "It was <u>just a fly</u>."

lament: (*luh-ment*) verb

to feel or express sorrow or regret for

- My little brother **laments** the loss of his toy car.
- I **lament** the day I decided not to go to school.

Synonyms: deplore, regret, bemoan, weep.

Antonyms: be happy, compliment, laud, praise.

Rhyme: lame gent

''I <u>lamented</u> the <u>lame gent's</u> condition and offered him some money.''

lavish: (*lav-ish*) adjective/verb

expended, bestowed or occurring in profusion (adj.)
to expend or give in great amounts or without limit (v.)

- King Edward invited everyone to attend the Princess's **lavish** wedding. (adj.)

- The King was **lavished** with gifts from all over the realm. (v.)

Synonyms: bountiful, effusive, excessive, generous.

Antonyms: austere, barren, scanty, stingy.

Rhyme: wish

''The fairy Godmother granted his <u>wish</u> for a <u>lavish</u> wedding.'' (adj.)

lax: (*laks*) adjective

not strict or severe; careless or negligent

- The robber broke into the bank easily because security was **lax**.

- The rules are quite **lax** in this school.

Synonyms: careless, indifferent, forgetful.

Antonyms: careful, caring, mindful, attentive.

Rhyme: tax

''You cannot afford to be <u>lax</u> about filling in your <u>tax</u> returns.''

lenient: (*lee-nee-uh nt*) adjective

agreeably tolerant; permissive; indulgent

- Being sent to bed without supper is **lenient** punishment.

- My mother was **lenient** towards me and my brothers; she let us watch T.V for an hour longer.

Synonyms: benign, compassionate, compliant, tolerant.

Antonyms: hateful, merciless, hard, intolerant.

Rhyme: lean on a tent

''The teacher was <u>lenient</u> because the boy did not mean to <u>lean on the tent</u>.''

liable: (*lahy*-buh l) adjective

responsible by law; likely to do or to be something

- "If you eat that many sweets, you're **liable** to get a toothache!" warned my mother.

- "Take my toys one more time and I'm **liable** to get furious!" my brother growled.

Synonyms: accountable, guilty, answerable, likely, prone.

Antonyms: irresponsible, unaccountable, excusable, immune.

Rhyme: label

"The dispatch clerk was <u>liable</u> for the mistake because he put the wrong <u>labels</u>."

lofty: (*lawf-tee*) adjective

extending high in the air; of imposing height; towering

- Rainforests are filled with **lofty** trees.
- The princess was locked in the **lofty** tower.

Synonyms: soaring, towering, tall, skyward.

Antonyms: below, beneath, humble, modest.

Rhyme: softy

"Although he was <u>lofty</u> he was really a <u>softy</u>."

majestic: (*muh-**jes**-tik*) adjective

having or showing impressive beauty or scale; of lofty
dignity or imposing aspect; stately; grand

- The Queen's palace is a **majestic** building.

- The lion is a **majestic** creature with thunderous roar.

Synonyms: awesome, grand, dignified, marvelous.

Antonyms: humble, low, shabby, lowly.

Rhyme: magic stick

''The little boy created a <u>majestic</u> castle with his <u>magic stick</u>.''

malicious: (*muh-**lish**-uh s*) adjective

full of, characterized by, or showing malice; intentionally harmful; spiteful

- The **malicious** trolls stole all the sheep from the poor farmer.

- Aurora was given a poisoned apple by the **malicious** Queen.

Synonyms: malevolent, wicked, evil, beastly.

Antonyms: aiding, assisting, decent, benevolent.

Rhyme: delicious

"The <u>malicious</u> minister put poison in the <u>delicious</u> meal before giving it to the king."

meagre: (*mee-ger*) adjective

deficient in quantity or quality; lacking fullness or richness; scanty; inadequate

- A million dollars is a **meagre** amount to a billionaire.

- The baker's assistant asked for a raise from his **meagre** salary.

Synonyms: insufficient, paltry, mere, little.

Antonyms: adequate, ample, enough, plenty.

Rhyme: my pet ogre

''<u>My pet ogre</u> thinks this meal is too <u>meagre</u>.''

mirage: (*mi-rahzh*) noun

something illusory, without substance or reality

- The old witch drank a potion and turned herself into a princess, a **mirage** of loveliness and beauty.

- The desert is dry and hot where a **mirage** of an oasis is often seen.

Synonyms: delusion, fantasy, hallucination, illusion.

Antonyms: certainty, fact, reality, truth.

Rhyme: my rage

''Imagine <u>my rage</u> when I realized it was not really a lake, only a <u>mirage</u>.''

modest: (*mod-ist*) adjective

having or showing a moderate or humble estimate of one's merits, importance; free from vanity, egotism or great pretensions

- Sally always won the national swimming race but she was always **modest**; she never boasted about her achievements.

- Stephen is from the village where he owns a **modest** house and a small farm.

Synonyms: humble, prudent, quiet, simple.

Antonyms: bold, ostentatious, vain, smug.

Rhyme: my desk

"I am not <u>modest</u>, so <u>my desk</u> is large to make me look important!"

nimble: (*nim-buh l*) adjective

quick and light in movement; moving with ease; agile; active; rapid

- The swift and **nimble** deer jumped over the sleeping lion.

- Tommy played the guitar well, he has **nimble** fingers.

Synonyms: adept, agile, lithe, quick.

Antonyms: awkward, clumsy, inept, slow.

Rhyme: fumble

"If you <u>fumble</u> over the hurdles the <u>nimble</u> person will beat you."

noxious: (*nok*-shuh s) adjective

harmful or injurious to health or physical well-being

- The poison ivy is a **noxious** plant.

- On our trekking trip we learnt about **noxious** insects, weeds and berries.

Synonyms: corrupting, destructive, fetid, harmful.

Antonyms: harmless, healthy, helpful, sterile.

Rhyme: cautious

''The police <u>cautiously</u> approached the <u>noxious</u> fumes coming out of the man-hole.''

oath: (*ohth*) noun

a formal and serious promise to tell the truth or to do something

- Jason the hero took an **oath** to always protect the city.

- Doctors take an **oath** to save lives.

Synonyms: affidavit, pledge, deposition, testimony.

Antonyms: break, kindness, silence.

Rhyme: sloth

"The <u>sloth</u> tried to take the <u>oath </u>to tell the truth in court."

I promise to tell the.......
mmmm.....????

oblique: (*oh-bleek*) adjective

not direct; slanting; sloping

- He issued an **oblique** attack on the President.

- The lines of a square should be drawn straight and not **oblique**.

Synonyms: bent, diagonal, inclining, leaning.

Antonyms: direct, parallel, perpendicular, level.

Rhyme: leak

''Because the pipe join was not straight but <u>oblique</u>, it was certain there would be a <u>leak</u>.''

obscure: (*uh b-**skyoo r***) adjective/verb

not readily seen, heard or understood; unclear (adj.)
keep from being seen; conceal (v.)

- Nate is on one of his adventures in an **obscure** corner of the world. (adj.)

- Grey clouds **obscured** the sun. (v.)

Synonyms: ambiguous, unclear, vague, mysterious.

Antonyms: clear, common, definite, known.

Rhyme: cure

"I'm afraid there is no <u>cure</u> for this <u>obscure</u> illness." (adj.)

obstinate: (*ob-stuh-nit*) adjective

difficult to change

- The devious thief was horrid, **obstinate** and perfectly rude.

- The old lady was taken aback by the **obstinate** child's behavior.

Synonyms: mulish, obdurate, unyielding, unbending.

Antonyms: submissive, tractable, pliable, amenable.

Rhyme: stain

''This ink <u>stain</u>, it is <u>obstinate</u>. I can't get it out.''

odor: (*oh-der*) noun

distinctive smell, especially an unpleasant one

- The **odor** of leaking gas through the summer breeze.

- Tammy pinched her nose at the, heavy and disagreeable, **odor**.

Synonyms: stench, whiff, stink, smell.

Antonyms: perfume, fragrance, scent, aroma.

Rhyme: a door

"The boy could tell from the <u>odor</u> there was something wild behind the <u>door</u>."

omen: (*oh-muh n*) noun

anything perceived or happening that is believed to signal a good or evil event or circumstance in the future; portent

- The dove is the symbol and **omen** of peace.

- Black cats are considered a bad **omen**.

Synonyms: portent, forecast, sign, premonition.

Antonyms: conviction, assuredness, sureness, fact.

Rhyme: old men

"The <u>old men</u> said the bird was a bad <u>omen</u> and the young man should not go on the journey."

oppress: (*uh-**pres***) verb

to burden with cruel or unjust restraints;
subject to a harsh exercise of authority or power

- Under the reign of the terrible dragon the people were **oppressed** with fear.

- The villagers were living in **oppression** under an evil regime.

Synonyms: maltreat, suppress, abuse, subjugate.

Antonyms: aid, assist, comfort, help

Rhyme: press

''The <u>oppressed</u> slaves were forced to work on the printing <u>press</u> all day and night.''

ordeal: (*aw-deel*) noun

any extremely severe or trying test, experience or trial

- One must wonder if children these days realize that life can be an **ordeal** sometimes.

- Climbing the Everest is quite an **ordeal**.

Synonyms: agony, difficulty, torture, torment.

Antonyms: comfort, joy, pleasure, happiness.

Rhyme: meal

''It is a real <u>ordeal</u> to eat this <u>meal</u>.''

ornament: (*awr-nuh-muh nt*) noun/verb

something used to beautify the appearance (n.)
to beautify; embellish (v.)

- ''Let's deck the halls with **ornaments** for the party!'' said my sister with glee. (n.)
- Famous scientists were called to **ornament** the university's conference. (v.)

Synonyms: adorn, decorate, garnish, beautify.

Antonyms: blemish, deface, mar.

Rhyme: argument

''They had an <u>argument</u> about the best place to hang the <u>ornament</u>.'' (n.)

passive: (*pas-iv*) adjective

not involving visible reaction or active participation

- The polar bear remains **passive** during hibernation, and takes no food.
- My mother remained **passive** while my brother and I fought.

Synonyms: apathetic, indifferent, resigned, stolid.

Antonyms: agitated, concerned, dynamic, lively.

Rhyme: massive

''The <u>massive</u> giant was <u>passive</u>.''

peril: (*per-uh l*) noun

exposure to injury, loss or destruction; grave risk; jeopardy; danger

- The knight saved his soldiers from great **peril**.
- They faced the **peril** of raging bulls.

Synonyms: hazard, insecurity, jeopardy, menace.

Antonyms: certainty, protection, safety, security.

Rhyme: pearl

''One of the <u>perils</u> of fishing for <u>pearls</u> is that you may be attacked!''

periphery: (*puh-**rif**-uh-ree*) noun

the outside boundary of any surface or area

- He dived into the blue lagoon from the **periphery** of the cliff.

- Tiny frogs sat on the **periphery** of the lotus leaf.

Synonyms: brink, fringe, perimeter, rim.

Antonyms: center, inside, interior, middle.

Rhyme: fairy

''The <u>fairies</u> danced on the <u>periphery</u> of the mushroom circle.''

perish: (*per-ish*) verb

to die or be destroyed through violence; decay

- The princess gave food to the villagers during the famine so that they will not **perish**.

- Many snails **perished** in the earthquake.

Synonyms: cease, crumble, disappear, pass away.

Antonyms: appear, arrive, build, grow.

Rhyme: cherish

''Quick!" she yelled, "Or the friends we <u>cherish</u> will <u>perish</u>.''

perplexed: (*per-plekst*) adjective

bewildered; puzzled

- ''What are you talking about?'' my brother asked **perplexed**.

- Sandy was **perplexed** by the puzzle; she didn't know how to solve it.

Synonyms: baffled, puzzled, uncertain, troubled.

Antonyms: certain, clear, sure, clarified.

Rhyme: relaxed

''The captain was <u>perplexed</u> by the passenger's <u>relaxed</u> attitude, when the ship was sinking.''

persevere: (*pur-suh-**veer***) verb

to persist in anything undertaken; maintain a purpose in spite of difficulty, obstacles, or discouragement; continue steadfastly

- The hero **persevered** up the high mountain to find the dragon.

- Several scientists **persevered** for several years to find a cure for the disease.

Synonyms: endure, hold on, keep going, persist.

Antonyms: cease, discontinue, give up, quit.

Rhyme: severe

''He <u>persevered</u> despite the <u>severe</u> pain and managed to win.''

perspire: (*per-spahyuh r*) verb

to secrete a salty, watery fluid from the sweat glands of the skin, especially when very warm as a result of strenuous exertion; sweat

- I always **perspire** after running a mile.

- The summer heat makes me **perspire**.

Synonyms: secrete, drip, exude, glow.

Antonyms: dry.

Rhyme: purse

''Carrying the heavy <u>purse</u> made the lady <u>perspire</u>.''

pioneer: (*pahy-uh-**neer***) noun/verb

a person who is among the first to explore or settle in a new place (n.)
develop or be the first to use or apply a new area of knowledge (v.)

- Mr Cadbury was the **pioneer** in chocolate research. (n.)
- The famous painter **pioneered** a new art form. (v.)

Synonyms: explorer, brave, head, inaugural.

Antonyms: secondary, following, last, late.

Rhyme: pie on ear

1: "How do you know he's a <u>pioneer</u>?" (n.)

2: "Because he's wearing a pie on his ear. He's a <u>pie on ear</u>!"

placid: (*plas-id*) adjective

pleasantly calm or peaceful; unruffled; tranquil; serenely quiet or undisturbed

- Benjamin is well-liked by everyone, he has a **placid** nature.

- The water may look **placid** but beneath it are dangerous creatures.

Synonyms: serene, easy-going, tranquil, quiet.

Antonyms: agitated, clamorous, disturbed, troubled.

Rhyme: acid

''He was <u>placid</u> when his book was attacked by <u>acid</u> because he already had another copy.''

pledge: (*plej*) noun/verb

a solemn promise or agreement (n.)
promise to do or refrain from doing something (v.)

- The new king **pledged** to build a stronger city for his people. (v.)

- The conference ended with a joint **pledge** to limit pollution. (n.)

Synonyms: agreement, assurance, oath, promise.

Antonyms: abort, breach, break, cancel.

Rhyme: ledge

''He made a pledge never to walk on a ledge ever again.'' (n.)

plume: (*ploom*) noun

a large, long, or conspicuous feather; in a shape resembling a feather

- **Plume**-filled pillows are my sister's favorite.
- The cowboy rode off into the sunset with a peacock **plume** in his hat.

Synonyms: quill, crest, feather.

Antonyms: There are no antonyms for plume (n).

Rhyme: plum

"Everyone at the <u>plum</u> party was wearing <u>plumed</u> hats."

plunder: (*pluhn-der*) verb

to rob of goods or valuables by open force, as in war, hostile raids, brigandage

- Pirates usually **plunder** from merchant ships.

- Ogres often **plunder** villages for treasure and trinkets.

Synonyms: loot, pillage, rob, ransack.

Antonyms: give, gift, deliver.

Rhyme: plunger

"They thought they could use a <u>plunger</u> to <u>plunder</u> the bank vault."

plunge: (*pluhnj*) verb

to cast oneself, or fall as if cast, into water, a hole; drop

- Tommy's Math grades keep **plunging**, he needs help.
- During hot summers we **plunge** into the lake for a swim.

Synonyms: dive, drop, fall, nosedive.

Antonyms: rise, ascend, climb, increase.

Rhyme: sponge

"The sponge man plunged into the water to rescue his friend."

pompous: (*pom*-*puh s*) adjective

characterized by a showy display of dignity or importance

- The **pompous** bully strutted up and down the hallway.

- The lawyer, who was nothing if not **pompous**, said he will get his client out of jail.

Synonyms: boastful, uppity, presumptuous, grandiose.

Antonyms: humble, kind, modest, simple.

Rhyme: compass

"He was so <u>pompous</u> he thought he was better than the <u>compass</u>."

poultry: (*pohl-tree*) noun

domesticated fowl collectively, especially those valued for their meat and eggs, as chickens, turkeys, ducks, geese and guinea fowl

- **Poultry** farming is tiring business.

- My uncle has a **poultry** farm in countryside.

Synonyms: duck, chicken, rooster, turkey.

Antonyms: There are no antonyms for Poultry.

Rhyme: poetry

"The <u>poultry</u> took part in a <u>poetry</u> reading circle."

precise: (*pri-sahys*) adjective

being exactly that and neither more nor less

- The cake has to be cut into 17 **precise** pieces, so that everyone gets an equal share.
- My sister told me to meet her at **precisely** 3.13pm.

Synonyms: actual, clear-cut, correct, definite.

Antonyms: ambiguous, easy-going, flexible, general.

Rhyme: size

''The <u>size</u> of the man, made the <u>precise</u> measurement of his weight impossible.''

prejudice: (*prej-uh-dis*) noun/verb

preconceived opinion not based on reason or actual experience (n.)
make biased (v.)

- It was felt that the news article could **prejudice** the jury. (v.)

- We should not hold a **prejudice** towards those different from us. (n.)

Synonyms: animosity, bigotry, aversion, intolerance.

Antonyms: fairness, love, tolerance, sympathy.

Rhyme: pre-judge

"The judge's <u>prejudice</u> against the poor caused him to <u>pre-judge</u> the situation." (n.)

privilege: (*priv-lij*) noun/verb

a right, immunity, or benefit enjoyed only by a person beyond the advantages of most (n.)
to grant a privilege to (v.)

- It was both a **privilege** and an honor to dine with the Queen. (n.)
- Schools with swimming pools **privilege** children who want to practice swimming. (v.)

Synonyms: advantage, benefit, entitlement, opportunity.

Antonyms: disadvantage, handicap, hindrance, loss.

Rhyme: village

''People of the <u>village</u> do not have the <u>privilege</u> of living in the big house.'' (n.)

prominent: (*prom-uh-nuh nt*) adjective

standing out so as to be seen easily; conspicuous; particularly noticeable

- Shooting stars are most **prominent** at night, but barely visible during daytime.

- Charlie's neon green shoes were the most **prominent** part of his outfit.

Synonyms: outstanding, arresting, beetling, easily seen.

Antonyms: common, ordinary, inconspicuous, obscure.

Rhyme: dominant

''His <u>prominent</u> nose is his <u>dominant</u> feature.''

provoke: (*pruh-vohk*) verb

to stir up, arouse, or call forth (feelings, desires, activity)

- Hearing the lone wolf's howl in the night would **provoke** fear in anyone.

- You shouldn't **provoke** a sleeping lion.

Synonyms: aggravate, anger, enrage, incite, produce.

Antonyms: alleviate, appease, calm, delight.

Rhyme: joke

''Even the jester's best <u>joke</u> could not <u>provoke</u> a smile on the face of the king.''

punctual: (*puhngk-choo-uh l*) adjective

strictly observant of an appointed or regular time; not late; prompt

- We were glad to be **punctual** for the first screening of the hit movie.

- Timmy is always late for practice, he is never **punctual**.

Synonyms: dependable, careful, accurate, early.

Antonyms: tardy, late, behind, overdue.

Rhyme: puncture

''We were all set to arrive on time but because of this <u>puncture</u> we will not be <u>punctual</u> after all.''

quaint: (*kweynt*) adjective

having an old-fashioned attractiveness or charm; oddly picturesque

- I love holidaying in **quaint** French towns.
- Jasmine shrubs have **quaint** little white flowers, but their scent is quite overwhelming.

Synonyms: bizarre, curious, fanciful, charming, attractive.

Antonyms: common, grave, normal, ordinary.

Rhyme: paint

''It looks old and quaint but we'll soon bring it up to date with a lick of paint.''

quell: (*kwel*) verb

to suppress; put an end to; extinguish

- Katie ran around the garden, unable to **quell** her panic, when she spotted a baby snake.

- Our apologies did nothing to **quell** our father's anger.

Synonyms: annihilate, conquer, extinguish, subjugate.

Antonyms: build up, compliment, encourage, help.

Rhyme: yell

''She <u>quelled</u> the invading ants with a loud <u>yell</u>.''

radiant: (*rey-dee-uh nt*) adjective/noun

bright with joy, hope (adj.)
a point or object from which rays proceed (n.)

- "What a brilliant day to go fishing!" my father exclaimed looking quite **radiant** in summer sun. (adj.)
- The diamond on the Queen's crown appears **radiant**. (n.)

Synonyms: beaming, brilliant, gleaming, glittering.

Antonyms: cloudy, dark, dull, gloomy.

Rhyme: radio ant

"The ant with the radio was <u>radiant</u> with joy." (adj.)

rank: (*rangk*) noun/verb

a social or official position or standing, as in the armed forces (n.)
to assign to a particular position, station, class (v.)

- A Colonel's **rank** is lower than that of a General's. (n.)
- Susan competed all over the world and was **ranked** the first among the contestants. (v.)

Synonyms: order, class, grade, position.

Antonyms: blighted, scarce, disorder, non-hierarchical.

Rhyme: bank

''The strange <u>bank</u> <u>ranked</u> their customers by their height.'' (v.)

recite: (*ri-sahyt*) verb

to repeat the words of, as from memory, especially in a formal manner

- We stay home, on rainy days, and listen to my sister **recite** poetry.

- My brother is fond of numbers and he would **recite** the timetable with ease.

Synonyms: chant, communicate, deliver, rehearse.

Antonyms: be quiet, conceal, keep, withhold.

Rhyme: re-write

"If you <u>re-write</u> it often enough you can <u>recite</u> it from memory."

reign: (reyn) noun/verb

the period during which a monarch occupies the throne (n.)
to possess or exercise sovereign power or authority (v.)

- Frank's **reign** of France lasted 100 years. (n.)
- Dwarfs have **reigned** the high mountains for hundreds of years. (v.)

Synonyms: dynasty, regime, tenure, administration.

Antonyms: weakness, incapacity, inferiority, subordination.

Homonyms: rain, rein.

Rhyme: rain

''The King celebrated 50 years of his <u>reign</u>. But the heavy <u>rain</u> cut short the celebration.'' (n.)

remorse: (*ri-mawrs*) noun

deep and painful regret for wrongdoing; guilt

- Feeling **remorse**, the thief gave back what he stole.
- Stricken by **remorse**, the evil Queen apologized to her people.

Synonyms: anguish, compassion, contrition, grief.

Antonyms: happiness, indifference, joy, meanness.

Rhyme: horse

''My horse felt remorse for knocking down his stable when he was upset.''

repent: (*ri-pent*) verb

to feel sorry for past conduct;
regret a past action

- The emperor, who was once cruel, **repented** his ways and became a great king.

- The headmaster told the bully to **repent** his horrid ways.

Synonyms: regret, rue, apologize, be sorry.

Antonyms: unapologetic, relish, revel, transgress.

Rhyme: re-paint

"Young man, if you <u>repent</u>, and <u>re-paint</u> the wall, we will not send you to prison after all."

residence: (*rez-i-duh ns*) noun

the place, especially the house, in which a person lives or resides; dwelling place; home

- Hotel Paradise is the best **residence** in Hawaii.

- Charlie has taken **residence** at the new mansion.

Synonyms: apartment, home, dwelling, domicile.

Antonyms: business, industry, office, space.

Rhyme: evidence

"There was <u>evidence</u> that the <u>residence</u> had been burgled."

restrain: (*ri-streyn*) verb

to hold back from action; keep in check or under control; repress

- Terry tried to **restrain** his tears but the fall hurt his knee too much.

- "Stop arguing and **restrain** yourselves!" said my mother to me and my sister.

Synonyms: confine, constrain, detain, restrict.

Antonyms: aid, allow, assist, permit.

Rhyme: restaurant

"They were <u>restrained</u> by the other diners in the <u>restaurant</u>."

robust: (*roh-buhst*) adjective

strong and healthy; hardy; vigorous

- Timmy isn't of **robust** health these days, he has been falling ill lately.

- Cindy wanted a **robust** doll for her birthday that would not break easily.

Synonyms: powerful, sturdy, tough, full-bodied.

Antonyms: fragile, incapable, weak, unstable.

Rhyme: robot

"The wall is <u>robust</u> enough to resist a <u>robot</u>."

rural: (*roo r-uh l*) adjective

of, relating to, or characteristic of the country, country life, or country people; rustic

- In some **rural** areas, people have no access to water.

- People are moving away from **rural** areas to live in big cities.

Synonyms: agrarian, bucolic, backwoods, agricultural, farming.

Antonyms: metropolitan, urban, city, suburban.

Rhyme: cruel

''The beautiful <u>rural</u> area can sometimes be <u>cruel</u>.''

seldom: (*sel-duh m*) adverb

on only a few occasions; rarely; infrequently; not often

- My mother **seldom** lets us watch cartoons at night.

- It **seldom** rains in the desert.

Synonyms: hardly, rarely, scarcely, sometimes.

Antonyms: frequently, regularly, often, usually.

Rhyme: shell kingdom

''In the shell Kingdom, you seldom see anyone wearing normal clothes.''

sermon: (*sur-muh n*) noun

a part of a Christian church ceremony in which a priest gives a talk on a religious or moral subject, often based on something written in the Bible

- Every Sunday my grandmother goes to church to hear the **sermon**.

- Tommy usually sleeps during the lecturer's **sermon** in class.

Synonyms: discourse, lecture, speech, preaching.

Antonyms: silence, speechlessness.

Rhyme: merman

"Down in the sea, a <u>merman</u> reads the <u>sermon</u>."

shrine: (*shrahyn*) noun

a special place in which you remember and praise someone who
has died, especially someone famous

- Every year my uncle goes to the **shrine** of Buddha in India.

- The king's remains were preserved in a **shrine** in the village chapel.

Synonyms: sanctuary, temple, sanctum, memorial.

Antonyms: There are no antonyms for Shrine.

Rhyme: mine

"They built the <u>shrine</u> in memory of the men who died in the <u>mine</u>."

sober: (*soh-ber*) adjective

serious, sensible, solemn; not drunk

- My sister is a morning-person; jumping out of bed in the morning bright and **sober**, ready to start her day.

- ''**Sober up**, sleepyheads!'' my father walked into our rooms with cymbals clanging, on a Sunday morning.

Synonyms: abstemious, composed, steady, sedate.

Antonyms: drunk, inebriated, agitated, irrational.

Rhyme: crowbar

''If he was <u>sober</u>, we wouldn't need the <u>crowbar</u>.''

soothe: (*sooth*) verb

to tranquilize or calm, as a person or the feelings; relieve, comfort, or refresh

- My grandma makes the best hot chocolate to **soothe** us on a cold winter's night.

- Lullabies **soothe** babies to sleep.

Synonyms: alleviate, pacify, relieve, lull.

Antonyms: aggravate, incite, provoke, trouble.

Rhyme: tooth

''He used the icepack to <u>soothe</u> the pain of his aching <u>tooth</u>.''

spectacle: (*spek*-*tuh-kuh l*) noun

anything presented to the sight or view, especially something of a striking or impressive kind

- While John enjoyed the **spectacle** of the acrobats, I was indulging in cotton-candy.

- The Romanian circus put on a spectacular **spectacle**.

Synonyms: comedy, display, event, performance.

Antonyms: hiding, expectation, normality, ordinariness.

Rhyme: crackle

"The <u>crackle</u> of the fire and the leap of the flames was a great <u>spectacle</u> for the onlookers."

stagnant: (*stag-nuh nt*) adjective

not flowing or running, as water, air; showing no activity

- Marla walked down the alleyway, wrinkling her nose at the foul smell of rubbish and **stagnant** water.

- Mosquitoes breed in **stagnant** waters.

Synonyms: dormant, idle, sluggish, filthy.

Antonyms: active, busy, energetic, moving.

Rhyme: stag and ant

''In a race between a <u>stag and an ant</u>, the ant appears <u>stagnant</u>.''

stallion: (*stal-yuh n*) noun

an adult male horse that is used for breeding

- Riding into town on his grey **stallion**, the hero was welcomed by all the townspeople.

- The equestrian, on her **stallion**, jumped over the hurdles with finesse.

Synonyms: horse, colt, mare, bronco, mustang.

Antonyms: There are no antonyms for Stallion.

Rhyme: tall lion

''The <u>lion</u> was so tall that he was mistaken for a <u>stallion</u>.''

stoop: (*stoop*) verb

to bend the head and shoulders, or the body generally, forward and downward from an erect position; lower one's morals to do something bad

- Because he was a very tall man he had to **stoop** to enter the house.

- At the edge of the woods a small house with low ceiling, even children had to **stoop** to enter.

Synonyms: crouch, bend, bow, sink.

Antonyms: rise, ascend, straighten, increase.

Homonyms: stoup

Rhyme: soup

''She <u>stooped</u> down to clean up the remains of the <u>soup</u>.''

stubborn: (*stuhb-ern*) adjective

unreasonably obstinate; difficult to move

- We always fight but my brother is too **stubborn** to relent.
- ''You are as **stubborn** as a mule!'' chided my mother.

Synonyms: adamant, determined, headstrong, relentless.

Antonyms: flexible, irresolute, complacent, compliant.

Rhyme: born

"He refuses to eat his food. This baby was <u>born</u> <u>stubborn</u>!"

sturdy: (*stur-dee*) adjective

strongly built; stalwart; robust

- Tall and **sturdy** walls were built around the kingdom to protect it from enemies.
- Extremely polite, he was a **sturdy** and valiant knight, one of the King's favorites.

Synonyms: bulky, burly, rugged, powerful.

Antonyms: delicate, feeble, tiny, wobbly.

Rhyme: wordy

''The table was not <u>sturdy</u> enough for such a <u>wordy</u> book.''

subdue: (*suh b-**dyoo***) verb

to bring under control; render submissive

- Bobby needed some medicine to help **subdue** the pain in his legs.

- Policeman Pat **subdued** the burglar.

Synonyms: defeat, quell, beat, tame.

Antonyms: release, incite, arouse.

Rhyme: stew

"The man on diet managed to <u>subdue</u> his desire to eat the <u>stew</u>."

submissive: (*suh b-**mis**-iv*) adjective

inclined or ready to submit or yield to the authority of another; unresistingly or humbly obedient

- The villain was **submissive** when he faced the super-hero.

- The new secretary is **submissive** to authority.

Synonyms: accommodating, deferential, obedient, tame.

Antonyms: disobedient, immodest, fighting, resistant.

Rhyme: massive

"The little puppy had no choice except to be submissive when faced by the massive wolf."

temperate: (*tem-per-it*) adjective

moderate in respect to temperature; showing moderation

- Many exotic fruits grow in the **temperate** regions of the world.
- Charles was **temperate** in his consumption of both food and drink.

Synonyms: agreeable, balmy, mild, restrained.

Antonyms: disagreeable, harsh, hateful, stormy.

Rhyme: temperature

"<u>Temperate</u> trees like a mild <u>temperature</u>."

thrifty: (*thrif-tee*) adjective

using money and other resources carefully, and not wastefully

- Backpacking through Europe taught me to be **thrifty**.

- I need to be **thrifty** and save money if I want to buy a mansion.

Synonyms: frugal, prudent, stingy, economical.

Antonyms: generous, wasteful, extravagant, uneconomical.

Rhyme: charity

''The <u>thrifty</u> millionaire donated fifty cents to <u>charity</u> on his birthday.''

torment: (*tawr-**ment***) noun/verb

severe physical or mental suffering (n.)
to afflict with great bodily or mental suffering; pain (v.)

- Billy the bully **torments** children in school. (v.)

- The defense lawyer **tormented** the witness with numerous questions. (v.)

Synonyms: agony, suffering, afflict, distress.

Antonyms: pleasure, joy, encourage, support.

Rhyme: tournament

"He was in <u>torment</u> having just lost the <u>tournament</u>." (n.)

trample: (*tram-puh l*) verb

to tread heavily, roughly, or crushingly

- Bobby and his new puppy **trampled** over mother's herb garden.

- People were running amok during the bison stampede to avoid getting **trampled**.

Synonyms: crush, encroach, flatten, squash.

Antonyms: aid, assist, help, improve.

Rhyme: trampoline

''The elephant had a tough time trying to <u>trample</u> ants on the <u>trampoline</u>.''

triumph: (*trahy-uh mf*) noun/verb

the act, fact, or condition of being victorious;
victory; conquest (n.)
to gain a victory; be victorious; win (v.)

- The rowing team's **triumph** brought fame and fortune to the city. (n.)

- Everyone believes that good will always **triumph** over evil. (v.)

Synonyms: celebration, joy, pride, elation.

Antonyms: disaster, failure, loss, sorrow.

Rhyme: three humps

''The winners of the <u>three humped</u> camel race celebrated their <u>triumph</u>.'' (n.)

trivial: (*triv-ee-uh l*) adjective

of very little importance or value; insignificant

- Swimming across the English Channel is no **trivial** feat.

- ''Do not bother me with **trivial** matters.'' said the Baron to his servants.

Synonyms: irrelevant, frivolous, minor, paltry.

Antonyms: consequential, important, meaningful, relevant.

Rhyme: aerial

''He wrongly thought walking the <u>aerial</u> high wire was a <u>trivial</u> challenge.''

turbulent: (*tur-byuh-luh nt*) adjective

being in a state of agitation; disturbed

- The rowdy, **turbulent** crowd was marching to the castle.
- Timmy's family has had **turbulent** times ever since his father lost his job.

Synonyms: stormy, unstable, tumultuous, rough.

Antonyms: calm, gentle, manageable, stable.

Rhyme: tub you lent

"This <u>tub you lent</u> me is useless in these <u>turbulent</u> waters!"

vacant: (*vey-kuh nt*) adjective

having no contents; empty; void

- Sarah likes to daydream, she often stares **vacantly** into nothing.

- Books fill a **vacant** mind with ideas.

Synonyms: bare, deserted, start, empty.

Antonyms: busy, full, occupied, aware.

Rhyme: vacation

"The sea-monster's presence resulted in the <u>vacation</u> homes becoming <u>vacant</u> quickly."

vicarious: (*vahy-**kair**-ee-uh s*) adjective

performed, exercised, received, or suffered in place of another

- Generals do not fight in the war, soldiers do, and their fame is attained **vicariously** through the soldiers.

- Jimmy's father always wanted to be a pianist but he couldn't, now he experiences the fame through Jimmy **vicariously**.

Synonyms: indirect, second-hand, substitute, surrogate.

Antonyms: first-hand, direct, primary.

Rhyme: victorious

''We were <u>victorious</u> not him. His victory is entirely <u>vicarious</u>.''

virtue: (*vur-choo*) noun

conformity of one's life and conduct to moral and ethical principles; uprightness; goodness

- The soldier's **virtue** and moral excellence led the King to anoint him as a Knight.

- Nuns are known for their **virtue** and compassion towards those who are less than able.

Synonyms: morality, ethics, honesty, integrity, rectitude.

Antonyms: vice, dishonesty, evil.

Rhyme: fur shoes

''The polar bears showed <u>virtue</u> by sharing their <u>fur shoes</u>.''

wholesome: (*hohl-suh m*) adjective

promoting health or well-being

- Everyone loves Amanda, she's a **wholesome** person.
- My mother's home-cooked **wholesome** meal fills my belly.

Synonyms: healthful, pure, nutritious, helpful.

Antonyms: dirty, unhealthy, bad, unwholesome.

Rhyme: stole some

"She <u>stole some</u> of my <u>wholesome</u> porridge!" said the little bear.

wretched: (*rech-id*) adjective

very unfortunate in condition or circumstances; miserable; pitiable

- What **wretched** weather we have in this city, it is always raining.
- I have a **wretched** lawyer who makes no progress in the lawsuit.

Synonyms: depressed, miserable, pathetic, woeful.

Antonyms: blessed, cheerful, nice, good.

Rhyme: wrecked

"She'd <u>wrecked</u> the car and it made her feel totally <u>wretched</u>."

Review Exercises

Review Exercise 1

Match the word with its definition.

(The first exercise has been done for you as an example)

_e_	1. **abrupt**	a.	more than enough
J	2. **absurd**	b.	to get something
A	3. **abundant**	c.	to say someone has done something wrong
H	4. **abyss**	d.	to choose someone or something as your own
C	5. **accuse**	e.	sudden and unexpected, often unpleasant
I	6. **accustom**	f.	to stick firmly to something
B	7. **acquire**	g.	having a lot of money or owning a lot of things
F	8. **adhere**	h.	a very deep hole that seems bottomless
D	9. **adopt**	i.	to make someone familiar with new conditions
G	10. **affluent**	j.	stupid and unreasonable, humorously silly

From the words above, fill in the blanks with the most appropriate word. (You may need to change the word form)

1. I could hear my coin clanking along the sides of the wishing well as it fell into the deep _Abyss_.

2. My hope is to _Aquire_ all the stamps I still need to complete my collection.

3. As we have several celebrities living nearby, our neighborhood is considered to be quite _affluent_

4. He left so _abruptly_ this morning that I didn't even have a chance to say goodbye.

5. Our teacher says we must _adhere_ to the school rules or else we won't be able to participate in after-school activities.

6. My sister _Accused_ me of eating the last biscuit from the tin, but it really wasn't true!

7. The large library had a/an _abundance_ of books.

8. It takes time to _accustom_ yourself to waking up earlier than usual.

9. It is _absurd_ to think that I would ever pass on the chance to take a trip to the seaside.

10. If we _adopt_ a more generous attitude towards each other, then the world could be a better place.

Review Exercise 2

Match the word with its definition.

__ 1. **aftermath**   a. a strong wish to achieve something
__ 2. **allocate**   b. to cause a particular feeling in someone
__ 3. **allure**   c. to give something to someone as their share
__ 4. **ally**   d. feeling worried about something coming
__ 5. **ambition**   e. someone who supports/helps another
__ 6. **ample**   f. to make a serious request for something
__ 7. **appeal**   g. the result and effects of an unpleasant event
__ 8. **apprehensive** h. to try to achieve something
__ 9. **arouse**   i. the quality of being attractive or interesting
__10. **aspire**   j. more than enough

From the words above, fill in the blanks with the most appropriate word. (You may need to change the word form)

1. To be fair, our mum tries to _____ chores to me and my three brothers equally.

2. I _____ to be a famous artist one day.

3. It's important that we have _____ time to prepare for our next exam.

4. The USA and Britain were close _____ in the World War.

5. Years later, the community is still struggling to recover from the _____ of the disaster.

6. The police are _____ to the public for information about the stolen car.

7. The music and enticing smells coming from my neighbors back garden _____ my curiosity.

8. The _____ of working in television was a strong factor in my career decision.

9. After many years of hard work, he finally fulfilled his childhood _____ to take part in the Olympics.

10. She felt extremely _____ about giving her presentation before all her teachers.

Review Exercise 3

Match the word with its definition.

___ 1. **asunder**   a. lost in thought, mildly amused
___ 2. **atrocious**   b. send someone away as a punishment
___ 3. **banish**   c. to not be loyal or to break a promise
___ 4. **barren**   d. of very bad quality
___ 5. **belligerent**   e. to surround a place / prevent people from leaving
___ 6. **bemused**   f. very confused, puzzled, not sure what to do
___ 7. **besiege**   g. wishing to fight or argue
___ 8. **betray**   h. into separate pieces
___ 9. **bewildered**   i. to think or worry about something for a long time
___10. **brood**   j. unable to produce or create anything new

From the words above, fill in the blanks with the most appropriate word. (You may need to change the word form)

1. We were _____ from the library for making too much noise.

2. The teacher was completely _____ by her student's attempt to cheat on the final exam.

3. I left my brother alone when I realized he was in a _____ mood.

4. The boat was torn _____ by the force of the hurricane.

5. My best friend tells me her secrets, because she knows that I would never _____ her trust.

6. The lack of rain for two months left the field of crops looking like a _____ wasteland.

7. My grandmother always said it was important not to _____ over past mistakes.

8. "That was the strangest joke I've ever heard," he finally said in a _____ way.

9. The movie was so _____ that I fell asleep in the first ten minutes of watching.

10. The celebrity was _____ by crowds of people as she left her hotel today.

Review Exercise 4

Match the word with its definition.

__ 1. **burden**   a. being honest / always telling the truth
__ 2. **calamity**   b. to gently persuade someone of something
__ 3. **candor**   c. someone with whom one spends time/travels
__ 4. **charred**   d. an accident or event causing suffering / damage
__ 5. **coarse**   e. to force or pressure someone to do something
__ 6. **coax**   f. partially burned
__ 7. **coincidence**   g. to be made up of
__ 8. **companion**   h. a heavy load or an oppressive, unpleasant duty
__ 9. **compel**   i. things happening at the same time by chance
__10. **comprise**   j. rough and not smooth or soft

From the words above, fill in the blanks with the most appropriate word. (You may need to change the word form)

1. I decided to put my shoes back on, for the sand felt quite _____ on my feet.

2. With great _____, she acknowledged that she was very bad at spelling.

3. My travelling _____ goes with me on all my international excursions.

4. In my failed attempt to barbeque at the party, I ended up _____ all the meat.

5. Vocabulary exercises _____ a large portion of my homework assignments.

6. Carrying the load of heavy books home from school was a _____ to the little boy.

7. Even though I was completely full, I felt _____ to eat the dessert that my mum spent hours making.

8. I am hoping that we can _____ my dad into taking us to the shopping mall today.

9. The flood that destroyed our home during the hurricane was a serious _____.

10. It was pure _____ that my friend and I wore the same outfit today.

Review Exercise 5

Match the word with its definition.

__ 1. **concealed**   a. someone too proud of their own abilities
__ 2. **conceited**   b. to secretly plan with someone to do wrong
__ 3. **condemn**   c. a strong feeling of dislike or disrespect
__ 4. **confine**   d. existing or happening now / modern
__ 5. **conspire**   e. express complete disapproval
__ 6. **contemporary** f. to decide according to law that someone is guilty
__ 7. **contempt**   g. to keep someone enclosed in a place
__ 8. **conventional** h. to match or be similar or equal
__ 9. **convict**   i. something prevented from being seen or known
__10. **correspond**   j. traditional and ordinary

From the words above, fill in the blanks with the most appropriate word. (You may need to change the word form)

1. When they were younger, the three brothers used to _____ with each other against their sisters.
2. The candy was _____ in her bag, so that her teachers wouldn't see it.
3. Some farmers attempt new methods of growing crops, but _____ methods often prove to be best.
4. You should _____ your parrot to his cage at night so he doesn't fly away.
5. Although they were sure he had committed the crime, there was not enough evidence to _____ him.
6. He is very disobedient to all the teachers and shows utter _____ towards them.
7. She sounded _____ when she told us that she was the smartest person in the class.
8. Classical music is nice, but I much prefer dancing to _____ music.
9. How well I did on my exam _____ with how much I studied beforehand.
10. Stealing and lying are universally _____ by all to be very bad things.

Review Exercise 6

Match the word with its definition.

___ 1. **covert**   a. to stop something before it is finished / to reduce

___ 2. **covet**   b. hidden or secret

___ 3. **coy**   c. to limit something that is not wanted

___ 4. **curb**   d. trick/cheat someone

___ 5. **curt**   e. to question someone about the work done

___ 6. **curtail**   f. to want something very much

___ 7. **debrief**   g. to refuse to obey or to challenge something

___ 8. **deceive**   h. a quick, rude reply

___ 9. **defy**   i. to be completely destroyed

___ 10. **demolished** j. playful secrecy or pretending to be modest

From the words above, fill in the blanks with the most appropriate word. (You may need to change the word form)

1. Having trained every day for two years, I aspired to win the _____ gold medal at our track and field competition.

2. It is sad to see so many children _____ their teachers by breaking the rules.

3. He gave a _____ reply when I asked him why he arrived so late.

4. The undercover spies were assigned a _____ mission.

5. The old, abandoned buildings were _____ to make room for the new shopping center.

6. When she realized her dad was watching her, the little girl blushed and gave a _____ smile.

7. The soldier was _____ after completing his assignment to obtain useful information from the enemy.

8. Due to lack of funds, the school must _____ some clubs and activities.

9. I feel bad about _____ my parents into thinking I was doing my homework when in fact I was watching movies all evening.

10. I find it very difficult to _____ my appetite when I see the delicious treats at the shop.

Review Exercise 7

Match the word with its definition.

___ 1. **depot**   a. a state of being confused, disorganized / untidy
___ 2. **derelict**   b. a feeling of losing hope / to lose hope
___ 3. **despair**   c. to give all your time to something or someone
___ 4. **despise**   d. a very untidy appearance of a person
___ 5. **devote**   e. a building where supplies or vehicles are kept
___ 6. **diminish**   f. a feeling of unhappiness and disappointment
___ 7. **disarray**   g. to feel a strong dislike for someone or something
___ 8. **disheveled** h. in bad condition, uncared for, run-down
___ 9. **dismay**   i. to spread across or move away over a large area
__ 10. **disperse**   j. to reduce or be reduced in size or importance

From the words above, fill in the blanks with the most appropriate word. (You may need to change the word form)

1. I _____ heavy metal music and do not understand how anyone could enjoy it.

2. Being forced to walk through the rain and mud, I looked quite _____ when I arrived at school this morning.

3. As the City Mayor, I will _____ myself to protecting the people of my community.

4. The abandoned, _____ house hadn't been lived in for five years and was a very ugly sight.

5. The crowd began to _____ when the show came to an end.

6. The number of beautiful flowers in our garden has _____ since the coming of winter's first frost.

7. She sank to the ground in _____ thinking she would never find her way home.

8. The fans were _____ when their team lost another match.

9. After a long day, the driver was looking forward to bringing the bus back to the _____ and heading home.

10. Since we moved home last week, everything has been in a state of _____.

Review Exercise 8

Match the word with its definition.

___ 1. **dispute** a. a feeling of extreme worry, sadness, or pain
___ 2. **distinct** b. a house or place to live in
___ 3. **distress** c. inactive, but can become active again
___ 4. **docile** d. clearly noticeable / notably different
___ 5. **dormant** e. a long period when there is little or no rain
___ 6. **dose** f. to not achieve something desired / to escape
___ 7. **drought** g. quiet and easy to influence or control
___ 8. **dwelling** h. to try to save money
___ 9. **economize** i. an argument or disagreement
___ 10. **elude** j. a measured amount of something

From the words above, fill in the blanks with the most appropriate word. (You may need to change the word form)

1. The doctor said she would begin to feel better after taking three _____ of the medicine.

2. The girl became very _____ when, after hours of searching, she could not find the lost kitten.

3. Our family has decided to _____ by not eating out and making more meals together at home.

4. This year a severe _____ has ruined our crops and dried out the rich soil.

5. There was a long-running _____ over who owned the land on the border between France and Spain.

6. The King's _____ was a huge castle with over 200 rooms.

7. Tourists enjoy the thrill of hiking across the _____ volcanos in Hawaii.

8. The gold medal continues to _____ me even though I've worked hard and want it more than anyone else.

9. I can always spot her in a crowd, for she has such _____ red-colored hair.

10. Our dog is extremely _____ and has never hurt anyone or disobeyed our commands.

Review Exercise 9

Match the word with its definition.

__ 1. **employ**　　a. to persuade someone by offering something
__ 2. **endeavor**　b. a short part taken from a speech, book, etc.
__ 3. **endure**　　c. to try to do something, make a strong effort
__ 4. **enterprise**　d. to say something or shout suddenly
__ 5. **entice**　　e. to build a building, wall, or other structure
__ 6. **erect**　　　f. to suffer something difficult or unpleasant
__ 7. **evoke**　　g. too much of something
__ 8. **excerpt**　　h. a business or organization
__ 9. **excess**　　i. to make someone remember / feel something
__10. **exclaim**　　j. to provide a job for someone and pay them

From the words above, fill in the blanks with the most appropriate word. (You may need to change the word form)

1. The smell of summer rain always _____ fond memories of my childhood.

2. After our flight was cancelled, we were forced to _____ a seven-hour delay at the airport.

3. An _____ of food can make you gain weight.

4. My dad's bakery is a private _____ which he named "Clyde's Cakes and Bakes".

5. "I can't believe you threw a surprise party for me!" he _____ with delight.

6. We need to _____ at least five more lifeguards if we want our pool timetable to run smoothly.

7. An _____ from her latest novel will be released in this weekend's magazine.

8. The delicious aroma of fresh coffee was so _____ that I had to buy a cup.

9. I am going to _____ to finish all my homework tonight so that I can go out with my friends this weekend.

10. The city council is going to _____ a memorial in honor of war veterans.

Review Exercise 10

Match the word with its definition.

__	1. **exhilarating**	a. extreme tiredness
__	2. **extract**	b. causing death/leading to disaster
__	3. **famine**	c. to make a deceptive or distracting movement
__	4. **fatal**	d. to take something out / to get information
__	5. **fatigue**	e. a group of ships / able to run quickly
__	6. **feeble**	f. weak and without energy, strength, or power
__	7. **feign**	g. able to produce or reproduce
__	8. **feint**	h. a severe lack of food in a large population
__	9. **fertile**	i. to pretend or fake something
__	10. **fleet**	j. making one feel very excited and happy

From the words above, fill in the blanks with the most appropriate word. (You may need to change the word form)

1. Sometimes I _____ paying attention in class when I am actually writing notes to my friends.

2. It was a heart-breaking moment when the doctor said that our grandfather's disease is _____.

3. My dad likes to tell the story of when he sailed in a huge _____ with the Navy.

4. To make olive oil, one must _____ the oil from the olives.

5. The soil in the countryside is so _____ that the farmers are able to grow a wide variety of crops.

6. Despite his _____, the athlete refused to stop running until he crossed the finish line.

7. We had the most _____ skydiving experience.

8. My teammate _____ a shot to the right, which confused the other team and allowed us to score.

9. It was kind of you to help the _____, old man cross the street.

10. Unable to find enough to eat, many people starved to death during the widespread _____.

Review Exercise 11

Match the word with its definition.

___ 1. **flora**   a. a small piece or part
___ 2. **flourish** b. to shred food against a rough surface
___ 3. **foe**   c. all the plants that grow naturally in an area
___ 4. **forbid**   d. rough and twisted because of age or weather
___ 5. **fragment** e. an enemy or rival
___ 6. **fraught** f. full of something undesirable
___ 7. **gene**   g. to grow or develop successfully
___ 8. **gnarled** h. the feeling of being grateful or thankful
___ 9. **grate**   i. part of a living cell that controls growth, etc.
___10. **gratitude** j. to refuse to allow

From the words above, fill in the blanks with the most appropriate word. (You may need to change the word form)

1. After being bitter _____ for many years, the two classmates finally decided to be friends again.

2. They were filled with _____ for all the wedding gifts they received.

3. We should avoid going through that neighborhood, because it is _____ with violent gangs.

4. There is an astonishing variety of _____ in the rainforest, including flowers found in no other environment.

5. Deep in the forest, we came across fantastic old trees with _____ trunks.

6. The librarian _____ us from making noise in the library.

7. "I'll make the pasta if you would please _____ the cheese to go on top", she said cheerfully.

8. After some time, the new student began to _____ in her new school, making friends and getting high marks.

9. The doctors concluded that the disease was caused by a defective _____ that he inherited from his parents.

10. My sister accidentally threw the ball through the closed window, and the ground became covered with _____ of glass.

Review Exercise 12

Match the word with its definition.

   __ 1. **grotesque**   a. a cheat, deception, or trick
   __ 2. **hoax**   b. rude and not showing respect
   __ 3. **ignite**   c. surgical opening made by a sharp instrument
   __ 4. **ignorant**   d. to cause something to start burning
   __ 5. **immense**   e. unable to be heard
   __ 6. **impede**   f. to prevent or delay something from happening
   __ 7. **impudent**   g. not having enough knowledge or information
   __ 8. **inaudible**   h. to encourage unpleasant or violent action
   __ 9. **incision**   i. strange and unpleasant, frightening or silly
  __10. **incite**   j. extremely large

From the words above, fill in the blanks with the most appropriate word. (You may need to change the word form)

1. I was _____ of the game's many rules, so it is no surprise that I lost.

2. Our phone connection was so bad that her voice was practically _____.

3. Dry wood _____ easily, so it is good for making a campfire.

4. His unpopular speech _____ the angry crowd to riot.

5. The _____ little child kept making rude gestures.

6. In the dark, the branches of trees assumed _____ shapes that gave me a creepy feeling.

7. The traffic is being _____ by the heavy rain.

8. At the end of the operation, the doctor stitched up the small _____ he had made.

9. The magician told me to pick any card as he started his elaborate _____.

10. The closer we came to the foot of the mountain, the more _____ it appeared.

Review Exercise 13

Match the word with its definition.

___ 1. **Inconspicuous**   a. not suitable as food
___ 2. **indulge**   b. to express sadness or sorrow
___ 3. **inedible**   c. to influence, move, or guide someone
___ 4. **inhabit**   d. not easily seen or not attracting attention
___ 5. **inspire**   e. to give a good reason for something
___ 6. **interpret**   f. large in quantity, expensive, impressive
___ 7. **isolation**   g. enjoy something desirable
___ 8. **justify**   h. being alone or separated
___ 9. **lament**   i. to live in a place
___10. **lavish**   j. to explain the meaning of something

From the words above, fill in the blanks with the most appropriate word. (You may need to change the word form)

1. I _____ my strange dreams as a sign that something bad was going to happen.

2. She accidentally left the stew on the hob for too long, so it ended up being completely _____.

3. In an attempt to _____ my actions, I explained that I had no other choice in the matter.

4. Some of the more remote islands are _____ by beautiful birds.

5. When my dad returned from abroad, he brought back _____ and exotic gifts for all of us.

6. He tried to look as _____ as possible so that he wouldn't be put in the spotlight.

7. The mourners _____ a life taken so suddenly.

8. Hearing about how she became an all-star player _____ me to follow in her footsteps.

9. I always look forward to my birthday when I can _____ in my favorite chocolate cake.

10. He's been living in _____ for so long that he has forgotten what it is like to have friends.

Review Exercise 14

Match the word with its definition.

__ 1. **lax**   a. an image that does not exist in reality
__ 2. **lenient**   b. beautiful, powerful, or causing admiration
__ 3. **liable**   c. without much care, attention, or control
__ 4. **lofty**   d. a very small amount or not enough
__ 5. **majestic**   e. to have legal responsibility
__ 6. **malicious**   f. simple, not large or expensive
__ 7. **meagre**   g. harmful or upsetting to others
__ 8. **mirage**   h. quick and exact in movements or thoughts
__ 9. **modest**   i. impressively high, noble in character or nature
__10. **nimble**   j. not as severe in punishment as expected

From the words above, fill in the blanks with the most appropriate word. (You may need to change the word form)

1. Our house may be _____, but it's all we can afford.

2. The new school is _____ when it comes to admissions standards, so it's beginning to get a bad reputation.

3. The _____, hidden waterfalls in the heart of the rainforest will leave you breathless.

4. How could anyone survive on a _____ diet of only bread and water?

5. We are being held _____ for the damages that we caused.

6. During our trip to the desert, we could see a _____ of a lake in the distance.

7. The mountain is so _____ that I don't know how we'll ever reach the top.

8. Preparing to attack his prey, the _____ cheetah moved silently through the terrain.

9. Given the severity of his crime, I believe that the judges were too _____ in their sentencing.

10. When I saw the _____ look in the man's eyes, it was clear to me that I could be in danger.

Review Exercise 15

Match the word with its definition.

__	1. **noxious**	a. a promise, especially one made in court
__	2. **oath**	b. an occurrence believed to predict the future
__	3. **oblique**	c. stubbornly refusing to change
__	4. **obscure**	d. to govern people in an unfair and cruel way
__	5. **obstinate**	e. an object that is beautiful rather than useful
__	6. **odor**	f. having a sloping direction, angle, or position
__	7. **omen**	g. a very unpleasant and difficult experience
__	8. **oppress**	h. poisonous or harmful (usually gas)
__	9. **ordeal**	i. a smell, often unpleasant
__	10. **ornament**	j. not readily seen or understood

From the words above, fill in the blanks with the most appropriate word. (You may need to change the word form)

1. After practice, the locker room had a foul _____ of sweaty feet.

2. Even after years of research, scientists still do not know everything about some of the more_____ planets in our solar system.

3. We usually decorate a fir tree with small, colorful _____ during the holiday season.

4. The witness took an _____ to tell the truth when she was called to the court.

5. The love of my family and friends sustained me through my tough _____.

6. Although my brother knows that he's wrong, he's extremely _____ and refuses to change his behavior.

7. Through her window came the last few _____ rays of evening sunshine.

8. For ten years, our people have been _____ by a ruthless dictator.

9. The _____ fumes from the chemical processing plant pose a danger to people living in the area.

10. Some people believe that black cats and broken mirrors are _____ of bad luck.

Review Exercise 16

Match the word with its definition.

__ 1. **passive**   a. to be confused or worried
__ 2. **peril**   b. the outer edge of an area
__ 3. **periphery**   c. to sweat
__ 4. **perish**   d. not active, allowing others to be in control
__ 5. **perplexed** e. having a calm appearance or characteristics
__ 6. **persevere** f. to persist determinedly despite obstacles
__ 7. **perspire**   g. a serious or formal promise
__ 8. **pioneer**   h. great danger, or something very dangerous
__ 9. **placid**   i. one of the first people to do something
__10. **pledge**   j. to die, to be killed, or cease to exist

From the words above, fill in the blanks with the most appropriate word. (You may need to change the word form)

1. The road we take to school in the morning runs around the _____ of the city.

2. We began to _____ as the hot summer sun beat down on us.

3. I felt that my life was in _____ when the black bears came into our camp.

4. I was surprised that he could maintain a _____ look on his face even as he was being scolded by the teacher.

5. Millions of people _____ in the World Wars.

6. Despite my exhaustion, I must _____ and keep going if I want to win this race.

7. The early _____ of modern medicine are responsible for developing many of the medicines we take for granted today.

8. My friend is normally so _____ about everything that it surprised me when he strongly protested against our plans.

9. At the wedding, the bride and groom _____ to love each other forever.

10. The students looked _____, so the teacher tried to explain once again.

Review Exercise 17

Match the word with its definition.

__ 1. **plume**   a. to move or fall suddenly, often a long way
__ 2. **plunder**   b. birds that are bred for their eggs and meat
__ 3. **plunge**   c. an advantage available only for some
__ 4. **pompous** d. to steal goods violently from a place
__ 5. **poultry**   e. famous and/or important
__ 6. **precise**   f. an unfair opinion not based on facts
__ 7. **prejudice** g. to cause a strong and often negative reaction
__ 8. **privilege** h. arrogant and full of self-importance
__ 9. **prominent** i. exact and accurate
__10. **provoke**   j. a large feather / tall, thin mass of smoke

From the words above, fill in the blanks with the most appropriate word. (You may need to change the word form)

1. Some _____ farmers keep turkeys and ducks as well as chickens.

2. It is unreasonable to hold a _____ towards strangers.

3. The pirates engaged in battle and _____ the coastal village.

4. There was a good turnout for my birthday party – fifteen of us to be _____.

5. Sometimes the older children get special _____ like getting to stay up past bedtime.

6. A _____ of steam arose from the place where the hot spring bubbled.

7. Because of its _____ position on the main street, the new bookstore will likely get a lot of customers.

8. He can sometimes sound _____ when talking about his acting abilities.

9. The bus fare was suddenly doubled which _____ an outcry.

10. We were so excited when we arrived at the beach, that we immediately _____ into the sea.

Review Exercise 18

Match the word with its definition.

___ 1. **punctual**   a. period of time a king or queen rules a country
___ 2. **quaint**   b. very happy or beautiful / giving off heat, light
___ 3. **quell**   c. to say a piece of writing aloud from memory
___ 4. **radiant**   d. arriving or happening on time
___ 5. **rank**   e. a feeling of sadness over something you did
___ 6. **recite**   f. a place where someone lives
___ 7. **reign**   g. something attractive in an old-fashioned way
___ 8. **remorse**   h. to say you are sorry and promise to change
___ 9. **repent**   i. to stop something / to suppress
___10. **residence**   j. a position in society or organization

From the words above, fill in the blanks with the most appropriate word. (You may need to change the word form)

1. My best friend cheered me up with her _____ smile.

2. He was so old when he took the throne that he only _____ for two years.

3. Recently the soldier has been promoted to the _____ of captain.

4. My classmate is so _____, that he arrives at the same time every day and has never been late to school.

5. Our assignment was to memorize and _____ the whole poem.

6. After our argument, I was filled with _____ and wished I could take back everything I said.

7. My family likes to stay in a _____ old cottage during the Christmas holidays.

8. When the criminal decided to _____, he vowed that he'd never do anything wrong again.

9. Extra police were called to _____ the disturbance.

10. The Queen does not spend the whole year in her official _____, as she enjoys travelling the country.

Review Exercise 19

Match the word with its definition.

__ 1. **restrain**   a. almost never
__ 2. **robust**   b. serious and calm or not affected by alcohol
__ 3. **rural**   c. strong and/or healthy, unlikely to break or fail.
__ 4. **seldom**   d. to make someone feel calm or less worried
__ 5. **sermon**   e. not flowing or moving (water or air)
__ 6. **shrine**   f. of or in the countryside
__ 7. **sober**   g. an unusual event that draws attention
__ 8. **soothe**   h. a religious/moral talk or speech
__ 9. **spectacle**   i. to hold back or restrict someone or something
__10. **stagnant**   j. a place built to honor gods, heroes, etc.

From the words above, fill in the blanks with the most appropriate word. (You may need to change the word form)

1. We witnessed the extraordinary _____ of an old lady climbing a tree to rescue her cat.

2. The most important item I need to pack for our hiking trip is a _____ pair of walking boots.

3. The young man created a _____ dedicated to his favorite football player.

4. Today's _____ at the chapel was on the importance of showing compassion to others.

5. The injured player was given medicine to _____ the pain.

6. After living in the city my whole life, I would prefer to settle in a quiet _____ area surrounded by nature.

7. My grandmother's funeral was a _____ affair, with quiet groups of people chatting politely around the room.

8. She was so angry that she could hardly _____ herself.

9. Two days after the storm, the _____ water puddles are still in my front yard.

10. I'm so busy with sports and school activities that I _____ have a moment to relax.

Review Exercise 20

Match the word with its definition.

___ 1. **stallion**   a. physically strong and solid or thick
___ 2. **stoop**   b. meekly obedient or passive
___ 3. **stubborn**   c. using money carefully
___ 4. **sturdy**   d. an adult male horse that is used for breeding
___ 5. **subdue**   e. mild weather or someone calm / controlled
___ 6. **submissive**   f. very determined and unwilling to change
___ 7. **temperate**   g. great suffering and unhappiness
___ 8. **thrifty**   h. to bring under control
___ 9. **torment**   i. to step heavily on something or someone
___10. **trample**   j. to bend the body forward and down

From the words above, fill in the blanks with the most appropriate word. (You may need to change the word form)

1. The demanding coach expected everyone on the team to be
    _____ to his authority.

2. The doorway was so low that we had to _____ to get through it.

3. He spent the night in mental _____, trying to decide what was
    the best thing to do.

4. The fire burned for eight hours before the fire crews could _____
    it.

5. _____ plants grow naturally in places where there isn't a hard
    frost or harsh sun.

6. The powerful _____ was so massive that I felt a little intimidated
    petting him.

7. I'm going to find out who _____ all over my flowerbeds!

8. I fear that the gnarled tree might fall during the next storm, because it is
    not as _____ as it used to be.

9. Although they have plenty of money, they still tend to be _____.

10. My brothers often have arguments because they're both so
    _____.

Review Exercise 21

Match the word with its definition.

___ 1. **triumph**   a. not filled or occupied, available for use
___ 2. **trivial**   b. a good, moral quality
___ 3. **turbulent**   c. a great success, achievement, or victory
___ 4. **vacant**   d. promoting health or well-being
___ 5. **vicarious**   e. in a state of agitation
___ 6. **virtue**   f. unpleasant or of low quality / very ill
___ 7. **wholesome**   g. having experience through someone else
___ 8. **wretched**   h. having little value or importance

From the words above, fill in the blanks with the most appropriate word. (You may need to change the word form)

1. Due to the rise in emergencies, the hospital had no _____ beds.

2. There is no reason to get upset over such a _____ matter.

3. A wise man once told me that patience is a _____.

4. One of the most important aspects of a healthy lifestyle is eating plenty of _____ food.

5. The two countries had an unpredictable and _____ relationship, which finally led to war.

6. She took _____ pleasure in her friend's achievements.

7. The game ended in _____ for the home team.

8. Since the earthquake, the people have lived in _____ conditions with no running water and little food.

Review Exercises: Answers

Review Exercise 1

Matching

1. e
2. j
3. a
4. h
5. c
6. i
7. b
8. f
9. d
10. g

Fill in the Blanks

1. abyss
2. acquire
3. affluent
4. abruptly
5. adhere
6. accused
7. abundance
8. accustom
9. absurd
10. adopt

Review Exercise 2

Matching

1. g
2. c
3. i
4. e
5. a
6. j
7. f
8. d
9. b
10. h

Fill in the Blanks

1. allocate
2. aspire
3. ample
4. allies
5. aftermath
6. appealing
7. aroused
8. allure
9. ambition
10. apprehensive

Review Exercise 3

Matching

1. h
2. d
3. b
4. j
5. g
6. a
7. e
8. c
9. f
10. i

Fill in the Blanks

1. banished
2. bewildered
3. belligerent
4. asunder
5. betray
6. barren
7. brood
8. bemused
9. atrocious
10. besieged

Review Exercise 4

Matching

1. h
2. d
3. a
4. f
5. j
6. b
7. i
8. c
9. e
10. g

Fill in the Blanks

1. coarse
2. candor
3. companion
4. charring
5. comprise
6. burden
7. compelled
8. coax
9. calamity
10. coincidence

Review Exercise 5

Matching

1. i
2. a
3. e
4. g
5. b
6. d
7. c
8. j
9. f
10. h

Fill in the Blanks

1. conspire
2. concealed
3. conventional
4. confine
5. convict
6. contempt
7. conceited
8. contemporary
9. corresponds
10. condemned

Review Exercise 6

Matching

1. b
2. f
3. j
4. c
5. h
6. a
7. e
8. d
9. g
10. i

Fill in the Blanks

1. coveted
2. defying
3. curt
4. covert
5. demolished
6. coy
7. debriefed
8. curtail
9. deceiving
10. curb

Review Exercise 7

Matching

1.	e
2.	h
3.	b
4.	g
5.	c
6.	j
7.	a
8.	d
9.	f
10.	i

Fill in the Blanks

1.	despise
2.	disheveled
3.	devote
4.	derelict
5.	disperse
6.	diminished
7.	despair
8.	dismayed
9.	depot
10.	disarray

Review Exercise 8

Matching

1.	i
2.	d
3.	a
4.	g
5.	c
6.	j
7.	e
8.	b
9.	h
10.	f

Fill in the Blanks

1.	doses
2.	distressed
3.	economize
4.	drought
5.	dispute
6.	dwelling
7.	dormant
8.	elude
9.	distinct
10.	docile

Review Exercise 9

Matching

1.	j
2.	c
3.	f
4.	h
5.	a
6.	e
7.	i
8.	b
9.	g
10.	d

Fill in the Blanks

1.	evokes
2.	endure
3.	excess
4.	enterprise
5.	exclaimed
6.	employ
7.	excerpt
8.	enticing
9.	endeavor
10.	erect

Review Exercise 10

Matching		Fill in the Blanks	
1.	j	1.	feign
2.	d	2.	fatal
3.	h	3.	fleet
4.	b	4.	extract
5.	a	5.	fertile
6.	f	6.	fatigue
7.	i	7.	exhilarating
8.	c	8.	feinted
9.	g	9.	feeble
10.	e	10.	famine

Review Exercise 11

Matching		Fill in the Blanks	
1.	c	1.	foes
2.	g	2.	gratitude
3.	e	3.	fraught
4.	j	4.	flora
5.	a	5.	gnarled
6.	f	6.	forbade
7.	i	7.	grate
8.	d	8.	flourish
9.	b	9.	gene
10.	h	10.	fragments

Review Exercise 12

Matching		Fill in the Blanks	
1.	i	1.	ignorant
2.	a	2.	inaudible
3.	d	3.	ignites
4.	g	4.	incited
5.	j	5.	impudent
6.	f	6.	grotesque
7.	b	7.	impeded
8.	e	8.	incision
9.	c	9.	hoax
10.	h	10.	immense

Review Exercise 13

Matching

1.   d
2.   g
3.   a
4.   i
5.   c
6.   j
7.   h
8.   e
9.   b
10.   f

Fill in the Blanks

1.   interpreted
2.   inedible
3.   justify
4.   inhabited
5.   lavish
6.   inconspicuous
7.   lamented
8.   inspires
9.   indulge
10.   isolation

Review Exercise 14

Matching

1.   c
2.   j
3.   e
4.   i
5.   b
6.   g
7.   d
8.   a
9.   f
10.   h

Fill in the Blanks

1.   modest
2.   lax
3.   majestic
4.   meagre
5.   liable
6.   mirage
7.   lofty
8.   nimble
9.   lenient
10.   malicious

Review Exercise 15

Matching

1.   h
2.   a
3.   f
4.   j
5.   c
6.   i
7.   b
8.   d
9.   g
10.   e

Fill in the Blanks

1.   odor
2.   obscure
3.   ornaments
4.   oath
5.   ordeal
6.   obstinate
7.   oblique
8.   oppressed
9.   noxious
10.   omens

Review Exercise 16

Matching

1. d
2. h
3. b
4. j
5. a
6. f
7. c
8. i
9. e
10. g

Fill in the Blanks

1. periphery
2. perspire
3. peril
4. placid
5. perished
6. persevere
7. pioneers
8. passive
9. pledged
10. perplexed

Review Exercise 17

Matching

1. j
2. d
3. a
4. h
5. b
6. i
7. f
8. c
9. e
10. g

Fill in the Blanks

1. poultry
2. prejudice
3. plundered
4. precise
5. privileges
6. plume
7. prominent
8. pompous
9. provoked
10. plunged

Review Exercise 18

Matching

1. d
2. g
3. i
4. b
5. j
6. c
7. a
8. e
9. h
10. f

Fill in the Blanks

1. radiant
2. reigned
3. rank
4. punctual
5. recite
6. remorse
7. quaint
8. repented
9. quell
10. residence

Review Exercise 19

Matching

1. i
2. c
3. f
4. a
5. h
6. j
7. b
8. d
9. g
10. e

Fill in the Blanks

1. spectacle
2. robust
3. shrine
4. sermon
5. soothe
6. rural
7. sober
8. restrain
9. stagnant
10. seldom

Review Exercise 20

Matching

1. d
2. j
3. f
4. a
5. h
6. b
7. e
8. c
9. g
10. i

Fill in the Blanks

1. submissive
2. stoop
3. torment
4. subdue
5. temperate
6. stallion
7. trampled
8. sturdy
9. thrifty
10. stubborn

Review Exercise 21

Matching

1. c
2. h
3. e
4. a
5. g
6. b
7. d
8. f

Fill in the Blanks

1. vacant
2. trivial
3. virtue
4. Wholesome
5. turbulent
6. vicarious
7. triumph
8. wretched

Word List

Abrupt	Absurd	Abundant
Abyss	Accuse	Accustom
Acquire	Adhere	Adopt
Affluent	Aftermath	Allocate
Allure	Ally	Ambition
Ample	Appeal	Apprehensive
Arouse	Aspire	Asunder
Atrocious		

Banish	Barren	Belligerent
Bemused	Besiege	Betray
Bewildered	Brood	Burden

Calamity	Candor	Charred
Coarse	Coax	Coincidence
Companion	Compel	Comprise
Concealed	Conceited	Condemn
Confine	Conspire	Contemporary
Contempt	Conventional	Convict
Correspond	Covert	Covet
Coy	Curb	Curt
Curtail		

Debrief	Deceive	Defy
Demolished	Depot	Derelict
Despair	Despise	Devote
Diminish	Disarray	Disheveled
Dismay	Disperse	Dispute
Distinct	Distress	Docile
Dormant	Dose	Drought
Dwelling		

Economize	Elude	Employ
Endeavor	Endure	Enterprise
Entice	Erect	Evoke
Excerpt	Excess	Exclaim
Exhilarating	Extract	

Famine	Fatal	Fatigue
Feeble	Feign	Feint
Fertile	Fleet	Flora
Flourish	Foe	Forbid
Fragment	Fraught	

Gene	Gnarled	Grate
Gratitude	Grotesque	

Hoax

Ignite	Ignorant	Immense
Impede	Impudent	Inaudible
Incision	Incite	Inconspicuous
Indulge	Inedible	Inhabit
Inspire	Interpret	Isolation

Justify

Lament	Lavish	Lax
Lenient	Liable	Lofty

Majestic	Malicious	Meagre
Mirage	Modest	

Nimble	Noxious

Oath	Oblique	Obscure
Obstinate	Odor	Omen
Oppress	Ordeal	Ornament

Passive	Peril	Periphery
Perish	Perplexed	Persevere
Perspire	Pioneer	Placid
Pledge	Plume	Plunder
Plunge	Pompous	Poultry
Precise	Prejudice	Privilege
Prominent	Provoke	Punctual

Quaint	Quell

Radiant	Rank	Recite
Reign	Remorse	Repent
Residence	Restrain	Robust
Rural		

Seldom	Sermon	Shrine
Sober	Soothe	Spectacle
Stagnant	Stallion	Stoop
Stubborn	Sturdy	Subdue
Submissive		

Temperate   Thrifty   Torment

Trample   Triumph   Trivial

Turbulent

Vacant   Vicarious   Virtue

Wholesome   Wretched

A note of thanks from the author

I hope you enjoyed reading this book and are benefiting from it.

This book has helped thousands of SSAT/ISEE aspirants improve their score and I look forward to hearing your personal success story!

Based on the tremendous positive feedback received, we have started work on the Second Edition of this book with more Vocabulary and more fun cartoons!

Please let me know how this book helped you improve, and as a special note of thanks for sharing your success story, we will give you a discount coupon for the Second Edition of this book when it comes out.

You can simply send your feedback to the email address below; sukhwibiz@gmail.com

Here is wishing you the best of luck with your learning!

(v6)

Made in the USA
Middletown, DE
12 March 2021